Musical Theatre for the Female Voice

Female musical theatre singers produce some of the most exciting and expressive singing an audience can experience. They also face a unique and specific set of issues when approaching their craft, from negotiating the registers of their voice to enable them to belt, to vocal health challenges such as premenstrual voice syndrome. This is the only book that offers a full and detailed guide to tackling those issues and to singing with full expression and technical excellence.

Musical Theatre for the Female Voice covers the origin of singing in musicals, from the bel canto style of 300 years ago through to the latest developments in high belting, in shows such as *Wicked* and *Waitress*. It offers the reader exercises and methods that have been used to train hundreds of singers at some of the UK's leading musical theatre training institutions and are underpinned by the latest academic research in journals on singing, psychology, and health. Every element of a singer's toolkit is covered from a female perspective, from breath and posture to character work and vocal health.

This is an essential guidebook for female singers in musical theatre productions, either training at university or conservatory level or forging a career as professional triple-threat performers.

Shaun Aquilina is a singer, director, and teacher. He has trained singers at the UK's leading musical theatre institutions such as GSA, ArtsEd, and Laine Theatre Arts. He is currently a Lecturer in Musical Theatre at Anglia Ruskin University.

Musical Theatre for the Female Voice

The Sensation, Sound, and Science, of Singing

Shaun Aquilina

LONDON AND NEW YORK

Cover image: peepo/Getty Images

First published 2023
by Routledge
4 Park Square, Milton Park, Abingdon, Oxon OX14 4RN

and by Routledge
605 Third Avenue, New York, NY 10158

Routledge is an imprint of the Taylor & Francis Group, an informa business

© 2023 Shaun Aquilina

The right of Shaun Aquilina to be identified as author of this work has been asserted in accordance with sections 77 and 78 of the Copyright, Designs and Patents Act 1988.

All rights reserved. No part of this book may be reprinted or reproduced or utilised in any form or by any electronic, mechanical, or other means, now known or hereafter invented, including photocopying and recording, or in any information storage or retrieval system, without permission in writing from the publishers.

Trademark notice: Product or corporate names may be trademarks or registered trademarks, and are used only for identification and explanation without intent to infringe.

British Library Cataloguing-in-Publication Data
A catalogue record for this book is available from the British Library

Library of Congress Cataloging-in-Publication Data
Names: Aquilina, Shaun, author.
Title: Musical theatre for the female voice : the sensation, sound, and science, of singing / Shaun Aquilina.
Description: Abingdon, Oxon ; New York : Routledge, 2022. | Includes bibliographical references and index.
Identifiers: LCCN 2022011467 (print) | LCCN 2022011468 (ebook) | ISBN 9781032261614 (hardback) | ISBN 9781032261591 (paperback) | ISBN 9781003286875 (ebook)
Subjects: LCSH: Musical theater--Instruction and study. | Singing--Instruction and study. | Women singers--Training of.
Classification: LCC MT956 .A75 2022 (print) | LCC MT956 (ebook) | DDC 782.1/4143--dc23/eng/20220310
LC record available at https://lccn.loc.gov/2022011467
LC ebook record available at https://lccn.loc.gov/2022011468

ISBN: 9781032261614 (hbk)
ISBN: 9781032261591 (pbk)
ISBN: 9781003286875 (ebk)

DOI: 10.4324/9781003286875

Typeset in Bembo
by KnowledgeWorks Global Ltd.

To the teachers who unlocked my voice:
Alex Ashworth
Dorothea Magonet

Contents

Acknowledgements viii

Introduction 1

PART I
Whole-Body Engagement 5

1 Posture 7
2 Breath 16
3 Voice 31
4 Vocal Health 55

PART II
Expressive Singing 65

5 Impression-Expression 67
6 Words and Music 89
  Final Thoughts 99

Index 102

Acknowledgements

I wish to thank the following colleagues, students, and friends, who gave their time to read the manuscript and provide feedback: Ryan Murphy and Adam Gerbertson, at ARU; Kirsty Nunn; Victoria Farrell; Georgia Farrow; and Andy Stevenson. I would also like to thank my family for their support and encouragement; the Surrey Institute of Education, particularly Professor Ian Kinchin for introducing me to Concept Mapping, Dr Marion Heron, and Dr Simon Lygo-Baker; Richard Harris for continued support, especially through the COVID-19 lockdown; Elsie Bastin and family for their support while I was training in London; Monique Morris and James O'Shea; and my formative teachers in MT, Sylvia Young, Ray Lamb, Peter Roberts, and Steven Baker.

Most of all, I thank all my students – this is for you.

Introduction

I'm always happy to meet a new student. Usually, you would walk into a small teaching room and I would greet you from the other side of the piano. Today, it's from the pages of a book. But it is a meeting no less and the beginning of our work together.

The goal of our work is expressive Musical Theatre singing. Expressive singing should connect with an audience, be exciting for you to create, and be healthy and reproducible for eight shows a week. To achieve that goal, we will explore the technical and artistic sides of your singing. Part I of the book deals with the technique: your physicality; how to engage your whole body when you sing; how to breathe; how to access your whole voice from chest to mix to head to belt; and how to stay vocally healthy. Part I is the groundwork that allows you to develop Part II. Part II is all about the artistic side and in that we will explore: expression; how to deliver meaningful words; how to unlock emotional sounds; what is a character; and how do you act on a character's intentions. There will be exercises along the way which will help you develop and practise all of this.

The subtitle of this book is "The Sensation, Sound, and Science, of Singing". These three perspectives have been used to train singers for hundreds of years. "Sensation" is what you feel physically as you sing; "sound" is what the listener hears, including pitching and tone quality; and "science" is the controlled investigations into the anatomical functioning behind singing. We will draw on all of these perspectives because each one supplies pieces of the singing puzzle.

We are part of a rich theatrical and singing tradition and I have tried to draw on that to give you a clear and efficient path to expressive singing. Everything in this book is either informed by my own singing, my experience of teaching top level students at UK conservatoires, the views of industry professionals, academic research, or all of the above. You will find frequent quotes supporting the ideas in this book

DOI: 10.4324/9781003286875-1

because it's important that you know those ideas are well-grounded in the expertise and research of others. We will also weigh the merits of those ideas. Sometimes, as in the discussion on breathing, I will suggest what I think is the best of way doing something, and other times, as in the discussion on character histories, I will leave it open to what you think works best for you. This is your book, now, and these are your lessons. Take what works for you.

This book is interested in the development of expertise. Expertise sometimes gets confused with talent but the belief in talent, that performers are "born with it", is and unhelpful and probably untrue.[1] I advise students to ignore talent and focus on effort instead. The performer who is concerned with effort, practice, and growth, will become better than the performer who is concerned with talent, achievement, and results.[2]

To become an expert, recent research suggests performers have to develop a sophisticated mental network of concepts which underpins what they do.[3] This is built up through years and years of practice, coaching, and performance. Once a performer has a highly developed mental network, putting it into action looks effortless (possibly giving rise to the belief that someone is "born with it").

In singing, there are several concepts in our network: posture, breathing, expression, words, tuning, rhythm, and more. Understanding how they work and how they interact can be mapped out. Here's Figure 0.1 my take on the network of concepts that underpins the expert singer's performance.[4] I hope by showing you this, you will have a visual representation of the kind of network we are trying to develop in you. At first glance, it might look confusing but don't panic. Read through it, tracing the lines that link one concept to another and look at the linking words that describe the relationship of one concept to another. We will explore every concept and how it fits into the network of singing over the course of this book (Figure 0.1).

As I said, when we watch a great singer perform, we only see the smooth working of that network. This can also be mapped. It's called a "chain of procedure". It's a chain because it goes from one action to the next. Figure 0.2 is what I think is going on in the procedure, or performance, of an expert singer.

As you can see, this is much simpler than the network. This expert procedure is what we are aiming for but to achieve it we have to recognise and develop the network of concepts that underlie it.

With all that said, let's begin. We start with Part I: Whole-Body Singing. Our first chapter is going to establish the foundation on which your expert singing will be built: posture.

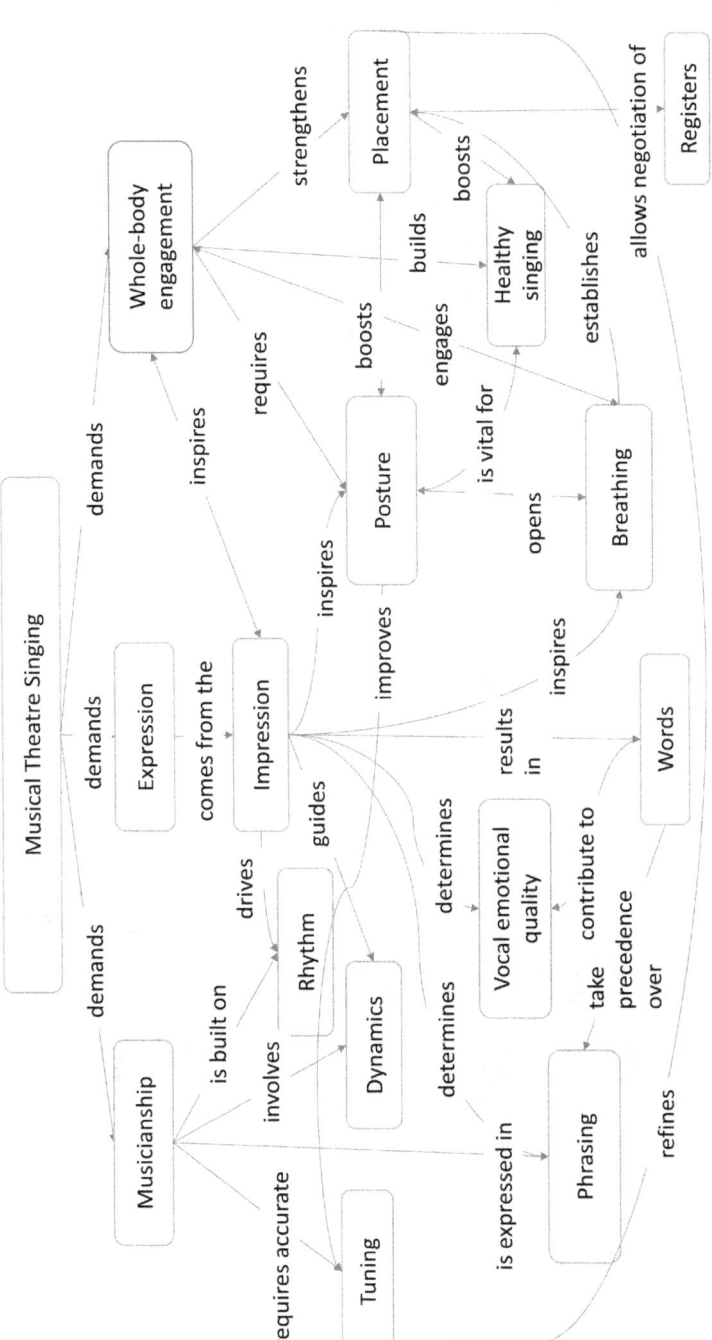

Figure 0.1 The network of singing concepts in the mind of the expert singer.

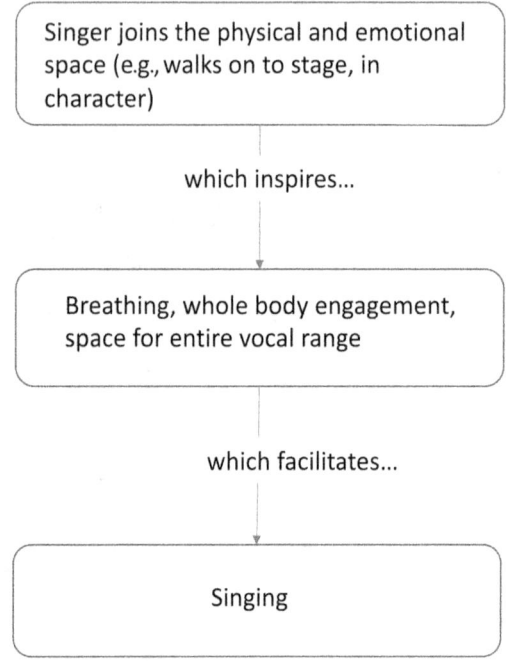

Figure 0.2 The "chain of procedure" of the expert singer, in performance.

Notes

1 Syed, M. (2011) *Bounce: The Myth of Talent and the Power of Practice*, Fourth Estate.
2 Dweck, C.S. (2006) *Mindset: Changing the Way You think to Fulfil Your Potential*, Random House.
3 Kinchin, I.M. and Cabot, L.B. (2010) *"Reconsidering the Dimensions of Expertise: From Linear Stages towards Dual Processing"*, London Review of Education, 8:2, 153–166.
4 For more on concept maps, their origin, and how they have been used, see Novak, J.D. and Canãs, A.J. (2007) *"Theoretical Origins of Concept Maps, How to Construct Them and Uses in Education"*, Reflecting Education, 3, 29–42.

Part I
Whole-Body Engagement

1 Posture

Posture is the foundation of your singing technique because so much else, such as range, placement, and belting, will be built on it. Get it right and everything else in your singing will come much more easily. Posture also gives you stage presence and is a part of the energised state of urgent communication that is singing.

To understand why posture is so important to the functioning of your voice, let's look back several million years to the development of the human voice. Our vocal system evolved when our ancestors walked on all fours. When they moved, their heads would lead and their bodies would follow. This produced a horizontal pattern of use that co-ordinated the muscles to function efficiently. (You can still see this in the movement of a pet cat or dog.) This co-ordination of muscles included the larynx and the voice. However, as the human race straightened up and walked on two legs, that co-ordination was disrupted. The head was now sitting on top of the spine and the body, creating a new upright support system. Co-ordinating this upright support system – in other words, creating good posture – is what will enable your voice to work at its best. Dr Theodore Dimon, in his book *Your Body, Your Voice* says, "When this [good posture] happens, the larynx and throat are perfectly suspended within this larger musculature, the ribs and trunk are supported to ensure proper breathing, and the larynx, ribs, and diaphragm coordinate perfectly to produce sound in a marvellously efficient way."[1]

When you think about posture, imagine it is something moving, rather than something fixed. Good posture is not static; it has an energised sense of direction, which expands and opens the body. You can open along the three dimensions of length, width, and depth. For example, you can lengthen up and down your spine, widen across your shoulders, and deepen between the front and back of your rib cage. This opens your posture and prepares you for singing. FM Alexander, the originator of the Alexander Technique, said "There is no such thing as a right position, but there is such a thing as a right direction."[2]

It is important to think of each of those directions as having its opposite, like a line with arrows at both ends, pointing away from each other. In their book, *The Alexander Technique for Musicians*, Judith Kleinman and Peter Buckoke emphasise that the use of opposite directions is vital: "It is the way we are designed to work. The head moves away from the feet, the feet move away from the head. The hands move away from the back, as the back moves away from the hands. The shoulders move away from each other."[3] As we focus on the parts of posture, remember that the whole posture has a sense of lengthening, widening, and deepening.

Let's explore our posture from the ground up, so that we really are engaging the whole body. As singers, we can be guilty of ignoring the bottom half of our bodies. We think plenty about the head, face, shoulders, rib cage, diaphragm, even the abs, and possibly the hips, but anything below that can be out of the mental picture. I want you to expand your mental picture down through your legs and feet and into the ground. That ground is solid and reliable. No matter how shaky you might be feeling, the ground is not going anywhere. (Remember this in auditions as it can help to settle your nerves.)

You are connected to the ground through your feet. More specifically, you are connected through three points: the ball of the big toe, the ball of the little toe, and the heel. Musician and Alexander Technique teacher David Nesmith compares it to a tripod:

> *The weight-bearing lower leg bone is at the front of the leg. Our weight is meant to deliver through this bone to the ankle at the apex of the arch. When we allow this to happen our feet support us like tripods, each foot delivering the weight down and back to the heel, and outward to each side of the ball of the foot.*[4]

This allows your weight to spread into the ground and create a sense of energy which springs back up into the body. It's another example of lengthening in opposite directions: you think down into the ground to come up to the sky. The subtle shifts between the three points of the foot also help give you balance. So, remember the old singing saying: sing from your feet!

Now that we have secured your dynamic connection to the ground, we can think of "stacking" your support. On top of your feet, you stack your ankles, knees, and hips. This, again, allows a feeling of strength to run through your legs in opposite directions: down into the ground and up into the hips. Singer Christine Isley-Farmer says "The knowledge that weight is transferred down through the hip joints into the femurs (thigh bones) through the bony structure of the lower legs into the feet aid[s] in the achievement of more balanced standing."[5] This balance will free your upper body to produce the singing sounds you are required to make. If you are singing Musical Theatre, you have probably trained as a dancer, as well. Dancers have strong leg muscles. Use them! All those years of ballet warm-ups can also help you sing.

Now we come to one of the most ignored areas of the body in Musical Theatre singing: the pelvic floor. The pelvic floor is a group of muscles at the base of your pelvis, that is between your hips, from the pubic bone to your coccyx (tailbone). These muscles help keep organs such as your bladder and uterus in place. For us as singers, they are vitally important for breathing and air flow. Musician David Nesmith writes, "This bowl of muscle at the base of the pelvis mirrors the diaphragm. These muscles, when allowed to be free, spring back during exhalation as a further aid to breathing. The resiliency of the abdominal wall and pelvic diaphragm are a tremendous auxiliary support to breathing."[6]

To locate the feeling of your pelvic floor muscles, you can try this exercise from the Royal College of Obstetricians and Gynaecologists:

> *Tighten your pelvic floor. You can do this by imagining you are desperate to pass urine and you are trying to stop yourself. Hold this for as many seconds as you can, up to a maximum of 10 seconds.*[7]

This exercise is only to make you aware of the muscles. It is not applicable to singing because, by tightening, it sends the muscles in the wrong direction. Singing requires a different engagement of these muscles. Christine Shneider began her career as an MT singer working professionally in New York, the US, and internationally. She has since founded The Visceral Voice and works as a manual therapist to help singers and other professional voice users. When I asked her about using the muscles of the pelvic floor for singing, she suggested thinking of them like a trampoline: "When you take an engaged breath to sing, your internal organs descend and the pelvic floor muscles receive and support those organs, much like a trampoline does when you stand on it."[8] Christine also emphasised that the pelvic floor works as part of a larger structure, akin to a cylinder, with the pelvic floor at the bottom, the diaphragm at the top, and some of the deep muscles of the lower torso wrapping around the middle.[i] This whole structure comes into play for

---

i Specifically, the transverse abdominus and the deep back muscles called the multifidus.

singing: "My focus with the pelvic floor is on timing, coordination, and integration."

The feeling you are looking for when you use your pelvic floor in singing should be a low, outward engagement and it should be strong, toned, stable, yet flexible, like a trampoline. As Christine also told me, the pelvic diaphragm is "responsive to each word" we sing, so it's active and dynamic throughout a whole song. If you sing with this depth of engagement, your sound will be healthier, richer, and easier to produce.

The pelvis can be thought of as the link between your top and bottom halves. We've dealt with the bottom so let's look at the top. We will start with the trunk. This is everything between your hips and neck: the abdominal muscles, diaphragm, rib cage and spine, and shoulders.

Do not concern yourself too much with your abdominal muscles. They should fill out a bit when you breathe but naturally so. Avoid "breathing into your belly". Trying to control your abs "can only lead to greater tension and actually interfere with breathing as a whole by getting the student to focus on all the wrong things," says Dr Theodore Dimon.[9] It is worth noting that this is an area where your dance training may hinder rather than help your singing training. Karen Hall, in *So You Want To Sing Music Theatre*, writes: "Dancers, for example, are trained to pull in the abdominal muscles in order to create a strong centre in the body for dance movement. This pulling in of the abdominal muscles often causes the intake of air to occur high in the lungs. The result is something we call clavicular breathing."[10] Clavicular breathing is breathing around your clavicle, also called collarbone. Essentially, the tension of your abs in dance sends your breath too high in singing.

If the pelvic floor is the most ignored anatomical part of singing, then the diaphragm is the part getting the most unwarranted attention. As a singer, you can ignore it, forget about it, and let it trouble you no more! Karen Hall says "it makes no sense at all to 'sing from your diaphragm'".[11] Dr Thoeodore Dimon adds, "altogether too much focus is placed on it by singers... it is in fact only part of a much larger system and can only work properly in this context."[12] By attending to your whole-body conditions, the diaphragm will take care of itself.

The word diaphragm comes from Greek and literally means "a partition across". It is a muscle that is "across" the bottom of your rib cage; what it partitions off is your chest (with your heart and lungs) from your abdomen. Your diaphragm goes up and down as you breathe but you cannot feel it. The muscle does not lead to any conscious sensation in your brain. What you can feel is the effect it is having on all those organs underneath it.[13] If you take a very deep breath and you experience a squashing sensation in your belly, that's the effect of the diaphragm pushing down.

The diaphragm is not even involved in all of your breathing. When you breathe out, the diaphragm is not active at all (hence Karen Hall's comment above). It is just along for the ride, returning to its ready position to breathe in. This is very important because, as Karen Hall says, "it makes no significant contribution to generating the pressure required to sustain phonation."[14] In other words, the breath you are singing on is not supported by the diaphragm at all.

What is supporting your singing breath is your pelvic floor (the "unyielding platform"), your rib cage, and your overall conditions. We will look at this in more depth in the next chapter, "Breath". For now, let's examine the role of the rib cage in creating your whole-body singing posture. The important thing to know here is that your larynx is suspended in a web of muscle. That suspension hangs down from the head and attaches to the sternum (breastbone). If you drop your rib cage or chest, you pull on those suspensory muscles and on your larynx. You can feel this if you put one hand on your chest, sing a soft "ooh" on one note, then drop your chest while you are singing. You will feel the effect on your throat (you might also notice the note goes flat – more on that phenomenon later). So, to keep the larynx in its most efficient working state, maintain the sense of opposite directions through the rib cage, allowing it to open by lifting, widening, and deepening.

The final part to mention in your trunk is your spine. This is another part of your anatomy that you can think of as lengthening in both directions. Avoid trying to straighten it out. Rather, use the natural curves that swing in and out. By connecting up to the skull, it should provide support and freedom for your head and neck.

We are now reaching the apex of the stack of support that started with the ground beneath your feet: your head and neck. Creating a structure that supports your head and neck is vital to your singing because it enables your larynx to operate freely and efficiently. You will not have to manipulate your larynx, it will produce the sounds you want because you have created the conditions for it to operate as it should. The whole-body structure also enables you to place your sound high and forward in your head (see Chapter 3). With this set-up, you can move elegantly through your head, mix, and chest registers, hit any note in your range on any vowel,[ii] and belt. The singer and teacher, Thomas Hemsley,

---

ii Any vowel, except at the very top of your head voice. There, the sounds are so high the vowels smudge together and lose their definition. We'll discuss this more in Chapter 3.

writes in his book *Singing and Imagination* that this apex of the structure should feel natural, co-ordinated, and free: "When the balanced adjustment of the neck and head is correct, the head *rests* on the end of the spine, and the neck *rests* on its base between the shoulders; the muscles of the neck and the organs and muscles within the neck are without tension… The head can be free to move in any direction without disturbing the balance of the vocal organs so long as the head is moved from the very top of the spine, not together with the neck."[15]

So, that's the structure for your whole body singing. Remember how to build it:

- ground
- feet
- legs
- pelvic floor
- ribs and chest
- spine
- neck and head

If you engage to this level, your singing will improve and you will create the conditions to progress to expert singing. Singing takes a lot of work, with your vocal folds vibrating hundreds of times per second to produce a sound. If you put all of that work on your throat, you won't be singing for very long but if you take that work and divide it up across your head, chest, and pelvic floor, you'll do much better. If you divide it even more to include your legs and feet, you'll be using as much of you as you can which means your singing can be produced with the utmost efficiency. Then you can sing freely and beautifully, for eight shows a week. When you get to an audition, you'll also have the chance of being a better singer than the person who is not using their whole body!

On "anchoring"

Before we move to the final element of posture, let's discuss a singing technique common in Musical Theatre training called "anchoring". I do not teach anchoring but it is worth exploring why it is taught and what its positives and negatives may be. The claim made in support of anchoring is that a rigid, tensed structure in specific parts of the body provides the best support for the larynx to produce and amplify sound. Gillyanne Kayes has written in depth about anchoring in *Singing and the Actor*. She says, "By anchoring the body we make a firm scaffolding for the vibrating mechanism of the voice and a solid resonating case for our instrument."[16] The muscles that provide this "firm scaffolding" are usually the bigger muscles in the neck and back. Typical exercises to develop the isolation of these muscles include imagining you are squeezing oranges under your armpits or placing your fist to your forehead and pushing against it.

Here are a couple more descriptions of anchoring, from *Singing and the Actor*:

- *"...you need to increase the work in the vocal tract and in the body to get more volume"* (p. 69).
- *"It is ok to feel your body is 'held', or braced, in the anchoring exercises, if you are feeling it around the back."* (p. 77).

The language around anchoring – *held, braced, solid, effort*, even the term *anchoring* – is difficult to reconcile with the language around whole-body singing – *open, lengthened, directed, free, energised*, and *easy*. It may be true that you need to do more physical work to get more sound but if you do that work with a well co-ordinated and efficient body, it should not *feel* like more work. On the contrary, it will feel smooth, gliding, like all the parts are synchronising to produce a unified result.

I disagree that it is ok to brace. Jerome Hines was an opera singer who sang at the top of his profession for more than 40 years. He wrote: "If you feel like you are weight lifting when you sing, it is wrong! Back off until the voice is floating and easy."[17] Thomas Hemsley CBE had an equally prestigious singing career. When he taught singing, he wrote: "Remember that everything I say assumes a well-grounded, *buoyant* posture."[18]

Anchoring may work for some people. My usual advice to students is to learn about it, try it, see if it works for you. Singing is not a precise science. Right and wrong answers vary for different people. But in my teaching experience, every time I have worked with a student on whole-body singing and released them from anchoring, they have sung better.

Tension right and wrong

Finally, I want to examine another vital element without which your singing structure will not work: tension. Tension has a bad reputation in singing. Who amongst us has not been picked up by a teacher for jaw tension, neck tension, shoulder tension? Some singers also have abdominal tension or tension in their knees. We are told to relax instead.

From this, we have extrapolated "tension bad, relaxation good." This is wrong. In singing, we are aiming for an energised state of high emotion, so we are clearly not aiming to be relaxed. Thomas Hemsley said "the word 'relax' is surely one of the most abused words of our time, particularly in singing studios."[19] We need, instead, to differentiate between two types of tension: static and dynamic.

"When somebody complains of tension, he really means too much tension, or, more precisely, the wrong *kind* and *amount* of tension, in the wrong *places*, for the wrong *length of time*."[20] So wrote, the musician and teacher Pedro de Alcantara in his book *Indirect Procedures*. This is what we mean by static tension. It almost certainly won't be cured by relaxing. Singing takes a great physical effort. If the right muscles are not employed to support it, your body will look for support elsewhere. That's when it will start tensing your jaw, shoulders, etc. So, static tension is a symptom of a different problem: the absence of the right support, the absence of dynamic tension. To release static tension, you have to redirect your body's efforts into the right place, at the right level, at the right time. This is dynamic tension and this is where those ideas of directing along opposite lines, of opening, lengthening, widening, and deepening, all find their place. They are dynamic tension: an attentive poise, ready to perform.

If you have performed dance routines in front of an audience, you will probably know the feeling of energy in your body in the silence before you begin. That's the feeling of dynamic tension. The three disciplines of Musical Theatre – acting, singing, and dancing – all have dynamic tension to varying degrees. It's usually seen as an increasing scale from acting to singing to dancing. Legendary director and choreographer Bob Fosse is reported to have said, "The time to sing is when your emotional level is just too high to speak anymore, and the time to dance is when your emotions are just too strong to only sing about how you feel." Stephen Citron, in his book *The Musical from the Inside Out* credits the critic Mark Steyn instead, quoting him as saying "when something goes beyond the spoken, it develops naturally into song; if it goes even beyond that, it goes into dance."[21] But here's the secret for you as performers: the dynamic tension of singing is not balanced midway between the two; it is much closer to that of dancing. That's the state you need to be in to perform.

Summing up

Good posture is the prerequisite of good singing. By engaging your whole body, feet to face, you set up the conditions for your voice to work efficiently, healthily, and beautifully. Posture is directional and it has a dynamic tension that infuses it with vitality. Now we move on to the animating material within your body: the breath.

Notes

1. Dimon, T. (2011) *Your Body, Your Voice: The Key to Natural Singing and Speaking*, North Atlantic Books, p. 9.
2. Alexander, F.M. (1974) *The Ressurection of the Body: The Essential Writings of F. Matthias Alexander*, New York: Dell Publishing Company, p. 4, quoted in de Alcantara 1997, p. 14.
3. Kleinman, J. and Buckoke, P. (2013) *The Alexander Technique for Musicians*, Bloomsbury, p. 66.
4. Nesmith, D. and Conable, B. (1999) "What Every Musician Needs to Know About the Body", *The Horn Call, The Journal of the International Horn Society*, 29:4 retrieved at https://www.bodymap.org/what-musicians-needs-to-know-about on 17/06/21.
5. Isley-Farmer, C. (2005) "Legs to Sing On: A Practical Guide for Singers and Voice Teachers", *Journal of Singing*, 61:3, 294.
6. Nesmith, D. and Conable, B. (1999).
7. "Your Pelvic Floor", *Royal College of Obstetricians and Gynaecologists* website: https://www.rcog.org.uk/en/patients/tears/pelvic-floor/ retrieved 17/06/21.
8. Schneider, C. personal email communication to author, 22/11/2021.
9. Dimon, T. (2011), p. 23.
10. Hall, K. (2014) *So You Want to Sing Music Theatre: A Guide for Professionals*, Rowman and Littlefield, p. 67.
11. Hall, K. (2014), p. 25.
12. Dimon, T. (2011), p. 23.
13. Watson, A. (2015), p. 7.
14. Hall, K. (2014), p. 25.
15. Hemsley, T. (1998) *Singing and Imagination: A Human Approach to a Great Musical Tradition*, OUP, p. 34–35
16. Kayes, G. (2000) *Singing and the Actor* A&C Black, p. 69.
17. Hines, J. (1997) *The Four Voices of Man* Limelight Editions, p. 33.
18. Hemsley, T. (1998), p. 43, my italics.
19. Hemsley, T. (1998), p. 28.
20. de Alcantara, P. (1997) *Indirect Procedures: A Musician's Guide to the Alexander Technique*, OUP, p. 15.
21. Citron, S. (1992) *The Musical from the Inside Out*, Elephant Paperbacks, p. 41.

2 Breath

Breathing for singing has been debated for centuries. There is evidence of singing teaching materials as far back as the year 535, when choristers were singing (well, at least chanting) in churches.[1] Despite the nearly 1,500 years since then, singers, teachers, scientists, and researchers still do not agree on exactly what is happening when we sing, nor what the best method is for singing, nor how we should go about training that method. What I will offer you here is what I have found to be the best method for me, as a singer, and for my students. I will also try to explain why I think it's the best method, continuing to draw on the work of highly regarded singers, teachers, and researchers.

Musical Theatre singing is part of the Western tradition of singing. Its roots are in classical singing such as opera, just like the roots of MT dance are in ballet, and MT acting is in classical acting like Stanislavski. These roots are a rich and exciting inheritance that has come down and belongs to you. It is your performing birthright.

They may sound different but both opera and Musical Theatre have plenty of similarities. They both require singers to perform songs with a broad vocal range, in a big theatrical space, often with large numbers of other singers and instrumentalists, in multiple performances. Today, some of the world's finest MT singers – Audra MacDonald, Kristin Chenoweth, Kelli O'Hara, for example – have a strong training in opera and classical singing, so it's worth knowing about on your journey to singing expertise.

The classical roots of singing really started to grow in the 1500s when teachers in Italy tried to record their methods. Some conventions still with us today, like breathing for a whole phrase and taking a silent breath, date back to this time. By the 1800s, two distinct ways of breathing for singing had appeared. One focused on lifting and opening the rib cage, and the other focused on lowering the diaphragm and breathing into the belly. Some people militantly committed themselves to one side or the other and swore the approaches could never be mixed; others were more chilled out about it and combined the two approaches.

Two key ideas emerged at that time that are still with us today: "appoggio" and the "lutte vocale".[i] Appoggio comes from the Italian word appoggiare which means "to lean". The sense is leaning down or resting on. Crucially, in singing, it includes the feeling that the thing being leaned on will come up by itself if allowed to do so. Jerome Hines, in *Great Singers on Great Singing*, explains: "I was confused by this until a picture came into my mind of trying to keep a rubber beach ball pushed under water. My push was the *appoggia* and the beach ball's buoyancy was the support. One exists because of the other."[2] When you sing, the diaphragm is the beach ball in you that wants to come up as you breathe out; the appoggio "push" feeling is your engagement right down to the pelvic floor. We'll be doing exercises on this, very soon.

The concept of appoggio is the root of what has now come to be known as "support". Some teachers believe the word "support" is a bad translation. It doesn't capture the dynamic balancing of two opposing forces. Therefore, instead of aiming for support, we will aim for whole-body engagement.

The other important idea, the "lutte vocale" is Italian for the "vocal struggle". It refers to the idea that as you sing, you should resist the deflation of the rib cage which usually occurs when you breathe out. Instead, you continue to use the muscles that help you to breathe in to create a counterforce to the muscles that help you to breathe out. This is still very much in use today and it is a big part of the system I will be using here.

Back in the 1800s, it was quite possible that the singers who breathed into their belly and focussed on lowering the diaphragm were the ones who came to value "appoggio", while the singers opening and lifting the rib cage valued the "lutte vocale". Both are part of co-ordinating your body to sing rich, expressive, healthy sounds and both are part of our whole-body singing.

There is another school of breathing that developed in England, which advocated pulling the abdominals in as you sing. This system is also in use in Musical Theatre today. Most singers and teachers are followers of one of these two techniques. The great American baritone, Sherrill Milnes, explains:

> Then comes the major difference in the schools of thought: the 'push in, squeeze in' school, or the 'stay out, pushing out' school, which I belong to.

---

i Pronounced "ap-PODGE-oh" and "LOO-ter vo-CAR-leh".

> *You can support by squeezing in. People do it and they are probably famous singers. I think the more efficient way is to expand the diaphragm and so forth all the way around the muscles. The maximum support from that expansion can be had by continuing the feeling of expansion through any musical phrase.*[3]

We are going to look at this kind of continuous expansion of breathing. It fits in with the ideas of expansive posture we discussed in Chapter 1, and I believe it is the most efficient and exciting form of breathing for singing. I also believe it aligns more closely with the emotional impulse of singing, which we will explore in Part II.

Let's take a closer look at the anatomy of breathing and how it applies to singing. No matter where you think about the breath going (abs, belly, chest), it really only goes into the lungs. Take a moment to place your hand on the area of your body where you believe the top of your lungs are. When I ask students to do this, I get a variety of responses from the bottom of the rib cage to somewhere level with the top of the armpit. Very few people go high enough (previous students who knew exactly where the lungs reach include an osteopath and a vet!). Put your hand on your clavicle (collarbone). The top of the lungs go right up behind that bone. When you were growing up, an early singing teacher may have told you not to breathe into this region at the top of the chest. It is what is known as clavicular breathing and it has been frowned upon since at least the late 1800s. The instruction to avoid breathing at the top of the chest is intended to prevent you snatching very high breaths that leave the rest of the body limp and unengaged. But this isn't the whole story. It is right that you should not *only* breathe into the top of your chest; it is wrong that you should not include that in your breathing *at all*. When you breathe, breathe into the whole of the lungs, including the top part. This is more efficient and more engaging. Remember how we discovered that your larynx depends on the lifted, open feeling of the ribs to function at its most efficient? Breathing into your whole lung space – including the top – is part of that. It prevents the chest from dropping or sagging, which pulls on the muscles of the larynx.

Now find the bottom of your breastbone, where the rib cage noticeably separates into two. Feel your way down both sides of the rib cage all the way round to your back. Your rib cage is a big structure and employing it in your singing is part of your technique. You should notice that the rib cage is lower in the back than in the front. It's important to keep that in mind when you think of lifting and opening the rib cage so that you really are engaging the entire structure. You can feel the opening of the lungs in the back through a simple exercise. Sit on a chair and wrap your arms around yourself, like you are giving yourself a big hug. Then, rolling down from the head, drop your body forward so your head is somewhere over your knees. Take a deep breath in that position and you should feel a delicious opening through the back of the lungs and rib cage.

Now we come to the fundamental physical issue about breath in singing: how it co-ordinates with the larynx to produce sound. First, let's picture the mechanics. Imagine a tube: air travels up the tube until it meets two long bands that act as covers across the tube. The air pushes against these covers until it builds up enough pressure to open a gap between them. Air passes through, the pressure drops, and the covers spring back because of their in-built elasticity and meet in the middle once more. Pressure starts to build up again and the whole process repeats. In this image, the tube is your trachea, or windpipe, the air is your breath, and the covers are your vocal folds. The opening and closing of your vocal folds creates a vibration in the passing air which is the first stage in your voice creating sound. (The second stage is resonance, which we will come to later.) You have to control that airflow because if you use too little air, the sound is thin and weak; too much and your vocal folds will either be strained or they will refuse to work altogether.

You can feel the effect of too much air on the vocal folds with a simple exercise. Put your hands on the side of your rib cage and sing a soft, sustained note. Now, press in your ribs, forcing more air through your throat. You should find the note disappears and there is only the sound of the air. This is because your vocal folds are very small, between 12.5 mm and 17.5 mm. (In men, they are longer, between 17 mm and 25 mm.)[4] They do not want a lot of air passing between them because they are too small to cope with that. Dr Theodore Dimon writes: "In this sense, the larynx isn't a wind instrument - that is, it isn't meant to be vibrated by forcefully blowing air through the glottis. When working properly, the breathing and the larynx automatically work together so that the vocal folds vibrate very efficiently with an absolute minimum of air pressure."[5]

So how do we create the right amount of air pressure? Remember, it is often said that singing takes less air than speaking. This is because to produce the long, sustained phrases of a song, we need to reduce the amount of air flowing between the vocal folds to an easy, steady stream which the folds can cope with. That takes a lot of control, especially since we are capable of sending through much more air than we need. Here's Karen Hall, again, author of *So You Want to Sing Music Theatre*:

"Healthy adults generally can generate more than twice the pressure that is required to produce even the loudest sounds; therefore, singers must develop a system for moderating and controlling air flow and breath pressure."[6] That system is going to be the outward, expansive feeling of breathing, which combines the concepts of the appoggio and the lutte vocale.

We are going to look at some exercises now. Before we do, there is a key point about this and any exercise you do for singing. Exercises are about working your whole-body singing. Whatever specific attribute the exercise is developing – singing a scale, controlling getting louder and softer, crisping up your diction – is secondary to developing your whole-body singing. That is the bit that demands work. Otherwise, you will go on learning exercises without ever realising the full potential of the system through which those exercises should be executed. FM Alexander wrote this back in 1941: "A person who learns to work to a principle in doing one exercise will have learned to do all exercises, but the person who learns just to 'do an exercise' will most assuredly have to go on learning to 'do exercises' *ad infinitum*."[7]

That being said, let us look at the exercises for appoggio. In the previous chapter, we identified the muscles of the pelvic floor. We are going to exercise these using voiced and unvoiced consonants. Voiced consonants use the vocal folds, like the "m" in "mother"; unvoiced consonants do not, like the "f" in "father". Remember you are looking for an outward, expansive feeling through the pelvic floor, not a tightening, pulling in feeling. If in doubt, give a small cough, without any harshness, and that should engage the right muscles in the right way. Take an unvoiced consonant, like "f" and say it eight times. Keep it rhythmic and strong, and try to locate the source of the sound in your pelvic floor muscles. Move on to these other consonants, and do the same thing:

- "k"
- "p"
- "s"
- "t"

This should give you a strong feeling of the consonants coming from your core. Singing consonants from your core is important for three reasons: (1) it will keep your body fully engaged as you sing; (2) it allows the consonants to be more expressive; and (3) it makes your words clearer to the audience. Never underestimate the value of these.

Once you have worked the unvoiced consonants, move on to the voiced ones and repeat the exercise. Voiced consonants you can use include:

- "b"
- "d"
- "g" – hard g, as in "golf"
- "m"
- "n"
- "v"
- "z"

Some consonants will be harder to connect to your pelvic floor than others. The hard "g" sound is often the one that gives students trouble. With practice, you will be able to start all your consonants from a deep-rooted place.

Next, extend the sounds over a longer period and maintain the feeling of connection in your pelvic floor. I would suggest the "v" and "z" sounds for this. Try a simple siren over a fifth, as shown in Figure 2.1, below.

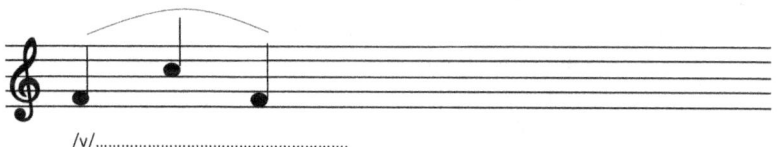

Figure 2.1 Exercise for low engagement: sliding up and down, over a fifth. This should be performed at different pitches, in a comfortable, mid-to-low area of your range.

Make sure you slide on this; avoid flicking from the bottom note to the top and back again. Do this around the middle and lower part of your range. Generally, I would not go higher than C5 (the octave above middle C).

A "rolled r" and a lip trill are both very good sounds for developing your low engagement. You can do this same exercise on those sounds, sliding over a fifth or going up and down a five-note scale. Some singers also find it helpful to do the exercises lying down semi-supine. If you want to try this, put some books under your head for support, and bend your legs so that your feet contact the floor but your knees are up. This can enable you to feel the deeper connection you are looking for.

Another good exercise for activating your pelvic floor and co-ordinating it with your diaphragm is panting. You can pant in three ways: (1) through your mouth; (2) through your nose; and (3) with no movement of air at all. Usually, this is also the order from easiest to most challenging. I would start with 30 seconds of each, with a few seconds rest in between, and then increase the time as you get stronger until you can do 45 seconds. The important elements are to keep the panting connected as low as possible and to keep it rhythmic. If it is juddery, it is not developing the level of control you want. This exercise can make people light-headed so be careful and stop if you feel that happening. Panting through the mouth can be a little drying on the throat so have some water to hand.

Once you have developed the feeling of low engagement in these exercises, be sure to carry it into your singing. You can practice a song on a "v", "z", rolled "r", and lip trill to strengthen your connection to the whole melody. Generally speaking, if you cannot lip trill a whole song, you shouldn't sing it in public. Develop the strength you need, first.

At this stage, this kind of training is simply muscle building; necessary, but not artistically interesting. We will get to the expressive, emotional triggers of this low engagement in Part II.

Now, let's turn to the lutte vocale exercises. It is a good idea to do these with your hands on the sides of your rib cage. That way you can measure whether the rib cage is expanding, collapsing, or staying the same. This is also a good exercise to do with a partner. You can experience the expansion or contraction of someone else's rib cage and provide them with feedback, and they can do the same for you.

The first of these exercises is Farinelli's Exercise. Farinelli, or Carlo Broschi to use his real name, was a famous singer in the 1700s. He was a castrato. That meant he had been castrated before reaching puberty so that he could retain the unbroken voice of a boy. The last musical institution to practice this was the Pope's Sistine Chapel, where the choir included castrati until 1902.[8] Farinelli was celebrated for his singing technique and the following exercise is attributed to him. It seems simple enough: you breathe in for a number of seconds, hold your breath for the same number, and breathe out for the same number. You then increase the number of seconds on each circuit of the exercise. The detail is the important part. In the middle section, don't think of "holding" the breath. As Richard Miller writes in one of his books on singing: "…one simply suspends the respiratory process. Breathing should be quiet and regular. Lips ought to be parted so that there is no holding back of the breath by the lips in the process. Aim for easy suspension of the breath, its measured exhalation, and for quiet breath renewal."[9] So, as you breathe in, you will feel the lifting, opening sensation of the rib cage and it's vital you continue that feeling as you suspend the breath and as you breathe out. This may feel counter-intuitive but you will develop the ability to allow the lungs to deflate while isolating the surrounding muscles and skeleton to maintain the feeling of opening. I would start with inhaling for three counts, suspending for three counts, and exhaling for three counts. Then increase to four, five, all the way up to eight. For speed, a metronome set between 60 and 68 beats per minute should be right. Remember to do this with your hands on your rib cage so that you can feel your expansion and check for its opposite, collapse.

Once you are building up the strength in your torso, you can combine the lutte vocale and the appoggio. Go back to your sustained appoggio exercises, like the sliding "v" over a fifth, and add in the feeling of the lutte vocale. The combination of feelings should have both the buoyancy and engagement of the pelvic floor and the expansion through the rib cage. Practise and you will find it. Remember: don't practise until you get it right, practise until you cannot get it wrong.

The in-breath

Let's now look at the action of taking a breath to sing. The in-breath should open up and engage your body in all the ways we have just explored: you breathe in to sing and immediately the pelvic floor engages and the whole rib cage lifts and expands. That way, your body is primed to make the sounds you (and the composer) want it to make. However, there's a secret here: the actions don't have to go in that order. You can do it the other way around. You can engage your core muscles and open the rib cage, and that action will draw the breath in. Instead of breathing, you can be breathed.

Let's explore that. If you stand with your excellent singing posture as described in Chapter 1, you can take an in-breath and trigger the feelings of expansion and engagement we've just worked on. However, now stand in the same way, with your mouth slightly open, and don't think about the breath at all but lift and open the chest and engage as low as you can. You should find that air comes in by itself. Now imagine you have something highly emotional to say, like you're finally confronting a bully. Imagine the courage needed, the importance of your message, and let that draw your posture upwards and open your body through the ribs, down to your core: can you feel the air coming in by itself? This is the idea of being breathed: the breath happens by itself. As Alexander said, "It is not necessary...even to think of taking a breath; as a matter of fact, it is more or less harmful to do so."[10] As long as you have a big emotional engagement, you can trigger the breath and the deep level of engagement demanded by singing. Low emotion situations won't do it. That's why in singing you have to be working at a high emotional level, because the material and your technique demand it. Then you can be rid of conscious thoughts about breath. These can interrupt what your body knows how to do automatically.

Once you are breathed for the start of a song, you can continue in that state for the whole song. The key is to maintain the opening, deeply engaged posture, between phrases. You can feel this when you do singing exercises. Do not allow any collapse of your posture at the end of a phrase or exercise. Instead, you stop singing, and that action of stopping will be enough to release the diaphragm and abs which draws air back into your body. It will feel like the abs spring back outwards. This creates an almost silent breath and avoids the gulping of air sometimes seen in singers. The springing back creates an easy cycle: you stay open, the breath comes in; then you sing out; then the breath springs back in; then you sing out. Singer Jerome Hines explains: "In a sense, you don't take the breath, it is taken for you. The sensation is one of relaxation, rather than that of a muscular effort. Therefore the attack in each phrase is preceded by a sensation of relaxation, rather than tension. This is in direct contrast to the common mode of breathing used in singing in which the breath is taken by a muscular contraction of the diaphragm and the attack is preceded by tension between the diaphragm and the abdominal muscles."[11]

All this again depends on your whole-body engagement. It is that structure which sets you up for these processes. Here's Dr Theodore Dimon: "The breath we need for singing, then, is already flowing in and out of our lungs, and understanding this is the key to preventing the habit of taking breath. You do not have to 'do' anything to get air into the lungs; it will come in and out by itself in the most efficient manner possible if you simply attend to the overall conditions on which breathing depends."[12]

So, now you can understand both breathing and being breathed. In performance, you will probably combine both to create a co-ordination of your body, breath, and emotions. The next element we need to add is voice.

Co-ordinating breath and voice

We have already looked at the process of air meeting your vocal folds and being vibrated by them to create sound. This process has two factors which determine how efficiently your voice works: (1) air pressure and (2) airflow.

Your lungs have what's called "passive pressure". That is, they have a certain pressure level just by virtue of being lungs, connected to a body, in an atmosphere with pressure and gravity. You can feel this with a simple exercise. Take a deep breath. Close your throat so no air can escape, like you're about to swallow food. Then relax your rib cage and all the surrounding muscles. It should feel like your body drops onto a buoyant resistance. That's the air pressure. Dr Stephen Austin, singer, teacher, and scientist, says that when we breathe in to sing, this in-built "passive" pressure is already big enough to push the air out so forcefully it would ruin our sound. That's where all the work we've done on appoggio and the lutte vocale come in. Dr Austin writes: "We have to 'check' these passive forces with active ones. We have to apply enough inspiratory force to take the excess pressure off of the vocal folds, so we use inspiratory muscles during exhalation (support) to balance the pressure."[13]

All this control of air pressure we have been exploring is great, unless it leads to too much control of airflow. Airflow is key to good singing so it's important that the work you do to control the air pressure does not also restrict your airflow. Air is part of the system that makes your voice work, like fuel is part of an engine: they both have to flow. The great American singing teacher, W. Stephen Smith, writes in his book *The Naked Voice*: "For singers to have freedom in their vocal production, they need greater airflow, not air pressure."[14]

So how do we make sure we're exerting the right level of control over the air pressure while also allowing the right level of airflow? I believe the answer is this. This part of singing is a two-stage process. The first stage involves setting up the body in a way that the pressure is regulated and the vocal folds won't struggle with too much air. The second stage — which is the one that historically doesn't get so much attention — is that, once that work is done, the air has to be free to flow within the system that has already been established, just like the fuel through the engine. Importantly, the fuel doesn't change the structure of the engine, and allowing the breath to flow shouldn't change your singing structure. Once your structure is secure, you must be liberal with the airflow. It's vital that the air moves because that is also part of making your singing voice work. Here's Stephen Smith again: "…in full singing it should still feel like we are releasing all of our breath all of the time. We actually *want* the sensation of losing our breath because that lets us surrender to the flow of air, thus feeling vulnerable and out of control. But in the process of letting go, we also gain the kind of power that only Free-Flowing Air can provide."[15] So, spend the air. Spend, spend, spend!

One of the other issues blocking the air from flowing may have to do with how singers were taught as children. Increasingly, I find many students were told they were breathy, when they were young. If you were breathy as a child, who cares? You were a child! Your body had years of growing and developing still to do before it was ready to really sing. International soprano and singing teacher Barbara DeMaio notes that breathiness in girls is an aspect of youth: "Prepubescent female voices present with a breathy tone that can continue through puberty and beyond."[16] She goes on to explain that it is part of the physicality of the female larynx to incline towards breathiness until the passing of puberty: "…research has shown that characteristic breathiness of the pubescent female voice is caused by a 'mutational chink', a gap between the arytenoids [two pieces of cartilage in the larynx to which the vocal folds are attached] caused by the growth of the larynx as it mutates during puberty; as the arytenoid cartilages grow, it takes time for them to harden and become strong enough to close the vocal folds fully. The mutational chink usually, but not always, disappears after puberty."[17] Unfortunately, labels like "breathy" stick, and young singers can still be concerned about them. My advice is to let that concern go. If you are doing all the postural work from Chapter 1, and the appoggio-lutte vocale work in this chapter, there is almost zero chance of you sounding breathy. There is, however, the chance of getting too tight, too rigid, and stopping the air from flowing. So let it go and let it flow.

Let's look at a simple exercise that can help you release your airflow. We are going to use a siren, which is very common in singing teaching. Sirens are essentially a long sound from somewhere near the top of your range to somewhere near the bottom of your range, on a specific vowel. You can siren from top to bottom, bottom to top, top to bottom and back again, and bottom to top and back again.

For this exercise, stand with your full, opening, and engaged posture, just as we described in Chapter 1. Remember, exercises are primarily about your overall conditions. If you're not training them, you will forever be learning exercises. On the in-breath, try to find the lowest engagement in your core muscles and the lifted opening of your rib cage. We are going to descend from very high to very low using the sound "ooh" like in the phrase, "Oh scooby doo, I wanna be like you-ou-ou." Go for a full "ooh" sound with very forward lips. For these particular sirens, the aim is not to produce a full, vibrant tone. The aim is to let the air flow. It should sound breathy. It should feel like the breath is rushing up through your body into your head. Once you feel that, try some from the bottom of your range to the top.

One of the key attributes this exercise develops is the sensation of making sound throughout your range without strain or static tension. In *The Naked Voice*, Stephen Smith says: "I do not care how high the pitch is, as long as people get there the right way – that is, without the sensation of resistance, with the airflow lifting the soft palate into a fluty, balloonish back space."[18]

When you get the hang of this exercise, you will start to differentiate the feelings of outward expansion and low engagement (stage one), and the easy, free, flow of the air (stage two). You need to develop both aspects to reach your singing potential.

Now that we've explored the in-breath and the journey of airflow through the body, let's talk about the air exiting the body. Whether you are singing or speaking, the air exits through your mouth. But the rate at which that air exits is very different for the two activities. Which do you think has the stronger rate of exit airflow, singing or speaking? The answer is speaking. You can prove this with a candle. Here's singer Jerome Hines, writing in *The Four Voices of Man*: "Try the classical experiment of speaking normally while holding a lighted candle about five inches before your lips. The flame will probably flicker, or even blow out. Relight the candle, and return it to the same position. Now produce a well-placed singing sound. This time, the flame should barely flicker... This experiment shows that you are using a smaller quantity of air in singing than in speaking."[19]

Another way of working this is to do a siren from high to low but this time on a lip trill. Place your hand a couple of inches in front of your mouth so that it's quite close. As you perform the lip trill siren, notice how much air you feel hitting your hand. How would you rate it on a scale of 1–10, with 10 being the strongest? There isn't much scientific method to this but when I ask students who are singing well where they rate their airflow, they consistently and reliably put it between 3 and 5. That seems to be the right balance.

When we sing, we generally want to produce a full sound that fills our performance space so let's explore the relationship of airflow to volume. Some schools of singing believe you need to increase your airflow to get more power.[20] However, in 2001, a study was published on this, called "Patterns of Breath Support in Projection of the Singing Voice."[21] The authors – who included the famous singing teacher Janice Chapman, originator of the **S**inger **P**lease **L**oosen **A**ny **T**ension SPLAT breath – studied five professional singers performing a song and asked them to vary how much they were projecting. The authors discovered that when the singers projected more, airflow went *down*. What increased was the intensity of their placement. We're going to discuss placement in the next chapter, but, essentially, placing the voice is focusing it in a particular area so that you feel that area vibrate, usually the area of the forehead between the eyebrows. When that happens, your voice is producing the tone you're singing and it is producing other frequencies above that tone. This is known as the singer's formant. It has long been held that placing the voice like this is what gives a singer power and enables her to be heard at the back of the theatre. So don't push your airflow in an attempt to be louder; trust your placement instead.

Onsets

Finally, it's worth considering the moment you begin to make a sound in singing, which is technically known as the "onset". Onsets are part of the craft of your singing, like choosing appropriate places to breathe or staying on pitch, so it's important to get them right. There are three types of onset and they sit on a scale, as shown in Figure 2.2, below.

Aspirate (breathy)   Balanced   Glottal

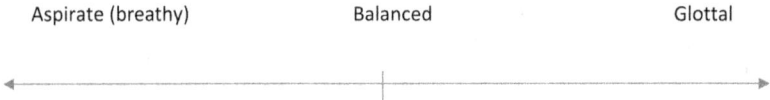

Figure 2.2 The onset scale. Singers should, generally, aim for the balanced onset in the middle, neither breathy nor glottal.

An aspirate onset starts a sound with too much breath. If you sing the vowel "ah" but put a breathy "h" in front of it so that it sounds like "ha", that's an aspirate onset.

A glottal onset uses your glottis. The glottis is the opening between the vocal folds. If you think of a word that starts with a vowel, such as "any", you can produce that first vowel with a small click in your throat. That's a glottal onset. This is the worst of the three because it puts a small strain on your vocal folds.

Between these two extremes lies the balanced onset, sometimes called the simultaneous onset. Here, you start a sound without breathiness and without the glottal click; there is only tone. This is the one we want for nearly all of our singing.

If you find you are prone to glottal onsets, use the aspirate onset instead. Imagine a lower case "h" in front of whatever you are going to sing and this should get the air flowing, alleviating the glottal onset.

Aspirate onsets can be the result of a lack of physical engagement. Make sure you are working your whole body before you begin a sound. They can also be a sign of trepidation, as if the singer wants to creep on to the note without anyone noticing. Be bold: stand and sing.

Summing up

Ideas about breathing for singing go back many hundreds of years. They form a long tradition of which you are now part. Getting the breathing right for singing first of all depends on your whole-body conditions. Then you have to balance the air pressure by maintaining an outward, opening feeling in the ribs and a deep engagement down to your pelvic floor. Once this first stage is established, you can run with the second stage, which is spending the air. Allow it to flow freely to co-ordinate breath and voice. The feeling of the breath exiting the body will be quite gentle. When it comes to increasing power, we look to placement rather than increased airflow. We, generally, begin sounds with a balanced onset.

After standing well in Chapter 1 and breathing well in this chapter, we have reached the point where you are making sounds. The workings of your voice, including its range, registers, and placement, are where we move on to in Chapter 3.

Notes

1 Lyle, H. (2011) "A Historical Look at Breathing Methods for Singing", *Voice and Speech Review*, 7:1, 310–317.
2 Hines, J. (1982) *Great Singers on Great Singing*, Limelight Editions, p. 222.
3 Ibid., pp. 174–175.
4 "Singing Science: How High and Low Can You Go?", *Scientific American* (2014) https://www.scientificamerican.com/article/singing-science-how-high-and-low-can-you-go/
5 Dimon, T. (2011) *Your Body, Your Voice: The Key to Natural Singing and Speaking*, North Atlantic Books, p. 32.
6 Hall, K. (2014) *So You Want to Sing Music Theatre: A Guide for Professionals*, Rowman and Littlefield, p. 28.
7 Alexander, F.M. *The Universal Constant in Living* (1941) quoted in de Alcantara (1997), p. 178.
8 Jenkins, J.S. (1998) "The Voice of the Castrato", *The Lancet*, 351: 1877–1880.
9 Miller, R. (2008) *Securing the Baritone, Bass-Baritone, and Bass Voices*, OUP, pp. 25–26.
10 Alexander, F.M. quoted in de Alcantara (1997), p. 98.
11 Hines, J. (1997) *The Four Voices of Man*, Limelight Editions, p. 30.
12 Dimon, T. (2011), p. 108.
13 Austin, S.F. (2005) "Two-headed Llamas and the *lutte vocale*", *Journal of Singing*, 62:1, 86.
14 Smith, W.S. (2007) *The Naked Voice: A Wholistic Approach to Singing*, OUP, pp. 40–41.
15 Ibid., p. 69.
16 Warwick, J. and Adrian, A. (editors) (2016) *Voicing Girlhood in Popular Music: Performance, Authority, Authenticity*, Chapter 5 "Girls and Puberty: The Voice, It's a-changin'; A Discussion of Pedagogical Methods for the Training of the Voice through Puberty" by Barbara Fox DeMaio, p. 99.

17 Ibid., p. 101.
18 Smith, W.S. (2007) *The Naked Voice: A Wholistic Approach to Singing*, OUP, p. 71.
19 Hines, J. (1997), p. 27.
20 See, for example, Kayes, G. (2000) *Singing and the Actor* A&C Black, p. 78: "Here's a summary of what you have learned to do so far: 1. Generate power from airflow…"
21 Thorpe, C.W., Cala, S.J., Chapman, J. and Davis, P.J. (2001) "Patterns of Breath Support in Projection of the Singing Voice", *Journal of Voice*, 15:1, 86–104.

3 Voice

Your voice is an amazing thing. It's capable of making all sorts of rich and exciting sounds. To make the sounds that meet the demands of songs and shows, we need technique and that's what this chapter will be about. Just like breathing in the previous chapter, there are different schools of thought on the best technique for singing. I'm going to continue on the path we've been travelling, as it meets all the demands of Musical Theatre (MT), is artistically expressive and rewarding, and can prepare you for a long and healthy career.

We're going to start by breaking up the voice into a few large segments known as registers. By understanding registers, we can understand how to use the voice efficiently and expressively.

The human voice doesn't sound the same at all pitches like an instrument does, such as a violin or clarinet. It sounds less like one voice and more like two or three depending on how high or low we are singing. These different distinctive sounds have come to be known as registers. This concept came about in the late 1700s in Italy. One of the earliest books on singing, *Practical Reflections on the Figurative Art of Singing*, was written by Giambattista Mancini and published in 1774. He defined two registers: (1) the "voce di petto" literally "voice of the chest"; and (2) the "voce di testa" or "falsetto" literally "voice of the head" or "false" voice. Over the next 250 years, the debate about registers continued and it centred on two elements: how may registers are there; and what method we should use to define them?

In the time since Mancini defined two registers of the voice, lots of other numbers have been put forward. After a career of top-level singing and interviewing several other singers, Jerome Hines decided there were four registers (hence the title of his 1997 book *The Four Voices of Man* – which also included the four voices of woman). In the 1860s, the German scientist and singing teacher Emma Seiler outlined five registers for the voice. But in 1887, the number defined by one of the most

DOI: 10.4324/9781003286875-5

important and best-known figures in the history of singing teaching was three. Mathilde Marchesi taught singing across Europe including cultural meccas such as Paris, Vienna, and Cologne. She only taught female singers, believing women should be taught by women and men taught by men.[i] She published many books, including *Bel Canto: A Theoretical and Practical Vocal Method*. In it, she writes of the importance of registers: "This is the Alpha and Omega of the formation and development of the female voice, the touchstone of all singing methods, old and new." [1] She goes on to write: "I most emphatically maintain that the female voice possesses three registers, and not two... The three registers of the female voice are the Chest, the Medium and the Head." If we replace "medium" with "mix", this is essentially how we can think of registers today.

When people in the singing world have defined registers, they have usually used three perspectives:

- the singer's physical sensations
- the sound produced
- the science behind the vocal mechanism

Soprano and singing teacher Kathy Kessler Rice explains this in her article on Emma Seiler:

> *Prior to the use of the laryngoscope while singing [invented in the 1800s], vocal registers had to be explained in subjective terms that relied heavily on the singer's sensations. Hence, each register claimed its name from its area of perceived resonation. One pedagogue in 1912 wrote the following description that aptly captured this mindset:*
>
> *The registers, like their corresponding resonance chambers, are three in number:*
>
> 1. *The chest register—reflecting the voice in the lower or upper parts of the chest.*
> 2. *The medium register—reflecting the voice in the lower or upper parts of the mouth.*
> 3. *The head register—reflecting the voice in the upper part of the head.*[2]

Later, teachers like Seiler and Marchesi used their observations of the larynx via the laryngoscope to refine their thoughts on the voice.

---

[i] My apologies to Mathilde.

It's important to know this because from these perspectives come much of the different vocal techniques and teaching we have today. We want to know:

- how does it feel when you sing: is it easy, free, strained, heavy
- how does it sound: rich, full, thin, in tune, flat, sharp
- and are you doing what the science tells us you should: engaging your core, opening the rib cage, etc.

I would say that all three of these need to be in play as you learn. An over-reliance on any one is in danger of leading you astray.

Today, the scientific perspective has led to a re-naming of the registers. Instead of "chest voice", you might hear the terms "thyroarytenoid dominant" (sometimes shortened to TA dominant), "thick fold", or "M1" (meaning Mode 1); while for head voice there's "cricothyroid dominant" (CT dominant), "thin fold", or "M2".[3]

Thyroarytenoid and cricothyroid are names for muscles in the vocal folds. Muscles sometimes take their name from what they are attached to. The thyroarytenoid is attached from your thyroid cartilage to your arytenoids. The cricothyroid is attached from your cricoid cartilage to your thyroid. When one of these two muscles is more engaged than the other, it is said to be "dominant". TA dominant singing bulges the vocal fold making it thicker, hence this way of singing is also referred to as "thick fold". CT dominant singing allows the TA to relax leaving the vocal folds longer and thinner, hence "thin fold". So CT dominant and TA dominant, and thick fold and thin fold, can be seen as two-register systems defined by the scientific perspective of what's happening at the level of the vocal folds.

The vocal "modes" is a four-register system defined by the scientific perspective of what's happening in the larynx. It distinguishes four distinct mechanisms in the larynx that produce sound. A study carried out in France and published in 2009 gives a very useful table for understanding this model (Table 3.1).[4]

Immediately, we can see a problem in applying this system to training singers. Look at the column for M2. It contains both your head voice and your mixed voice. But singers definitely feel a difference between those two registers and there's a difference in sound. As Marchesi said, students find "their own experience teaches them after a few lessons"[5] that these registers are different. In *The Naked Voice*, Stephen Smith says "...scientific analysis can only tell us what *happens* when we sing. It cannot tell us what we must *do* to sing well."[6] We will be concerned with what you need to do. An overview of these terms and where they

34 Whole-Body Engagement

Table 3.1 The vocal modes. This table uses the four vocal modes to categorise common terms for vocal registers

M0	M1	M2	M3
[Vocal] Fry	Modal	Falsetto	Whistle
Pulse	Normal	Head (women)	Flageolet
Strohbass	Chest	Loft	Flute
Voix de Contrabasse	Heavy	Light	Sifflet
	Thick	Thin	
	Voix Mixte (men)	Voix Mixte (women)	
	Mixed (men)	Mixed (women)	
	Voce finta (men)		
	Head operatic (men)		

Source: Roubeau, Henrich, and Castellengo, 2009.

come from is useful. For example, a musical director might ask you to sing a phrase more in thin fold, in which case you just need to know that means more in head voice. But by using the terms chest, mix, and head, we will be able to successfully navigate all the areas of your voice and find a route that will take us to healthy and exciting belting.

Let's look now at the approximate range of each register. Figure 3.1 shows how an MT soprano would define their registers on the piano:

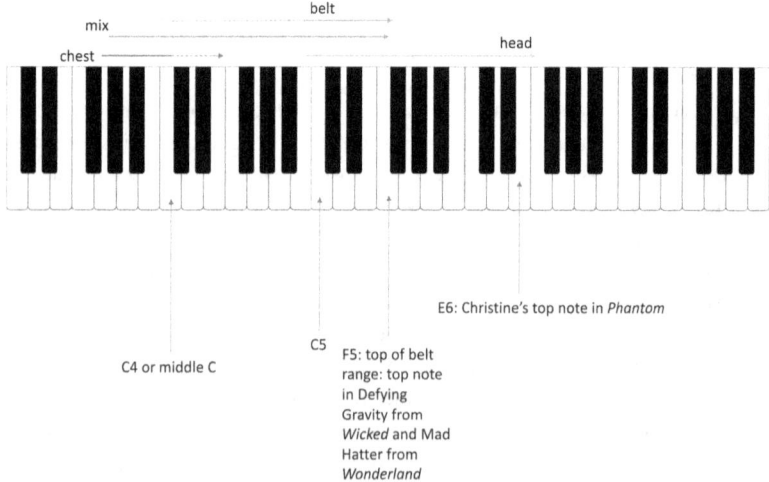

Figure 3.1 The approximate range and registers of an MT soprano.

Note the overlaps. The mixed voice overlaps with almost all the chest voice and some singers never use pure chest. Mix also overlaps with belt and with head. The note C5 is where a lot of female singers want to flip from their mix into their head. That dotted line on the chest shows where you can take your chest up to but singers almost never do because it sounds strained and makes switching into mix much more difficult and clunky.

Figure 3.2 shows the range and registers, on the same section of the piano, of mezzos/altos.

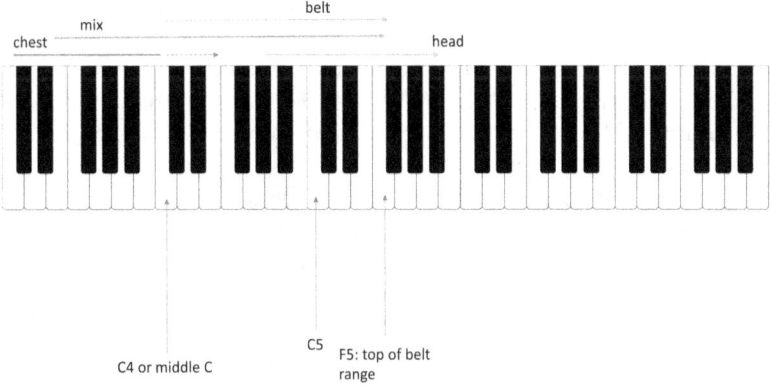

Figure 3.2 The approximate range and registers of an MT mezzo/alto.

There's clearly much more going on at the bottom for altos and mezzos.[ii] Notice the lower head voice as well. The area of change from mix to head will be slightly lower for mezzos/altos, as well, anywhere from Ab4 to C5.

The important things about registers are knowing where they are, how to access them, and how to move between them smoothly. Let's explore that now.

Where are your registers?

The terms head, mix, and chest refer to the sensations you feel when you use your voice. Usually, you will feel vibrations in your chest when singing low and in your head when singing high. Mix should

---

ii The Guiness World Record for the lowest note sung by a female is D2(!) and goes to Helen Leahey from Wales.

feel like both at the same time. You can try this by putting one hand on your chest and the other on your forehead and performing sirens from very low to very high and back, on the vowel "oo". You can feel the sensations moving around in tandem with the pitch of the siren.

Many singers don't get down into their chest voice, especially if they are a soprano. To make sure you are reaching your chest, start by speaking the vowel "ee" at the bottom of your voice. No singing, just speak it. Then speak it for a long time: "eeeeeeeeeeee". That should be your chest voice. It might take some effort to stay there and not slip into your mix. It's difficult to hear pure chest voice on recordings because it is so very rarely used – you can see by the overlaps on the diagrams that mix will cover most of the same notes. However, listen to Patina Miller's performance of "Simple Joys" from the New Broadway Cast Recording of *Pippin*. In the first 30 seconds you'll hear a much chestier sound moving smoothly to a mix.

Your head voice is much easier to identify: it's the really high stuff. The tricky part is often to tell the difference between your head and your mix, especially as you move upwards note by note. Practise sirens, both up and down, and try to notice when you think you are changing. I often ask students to do this and to raise their hand when they think they have shifted register. Sometimes they know where it's happening and sometimes not. A teacher's ears are invaluable here.

You can listen to an example of changing from head to mix in Sierra Boggess's Original Cast Recording of "Love Never Dies" from *Love Never Dies*. The title phrase often has two notes in head – "Love ne-" – and two notes in mix – "-ver dies".

That leaves your mixed voice. This is where you will spend most of your time in Musical Theatre singing. It's a mix of your head and chest and, as with any mixture, the amounts you put in can vary. You can have a chestier mix lower in your voice and a headier mix higher in your voice. The really important thing to note is this: the higher you go in your mix, the more chest you have to release. If you try to hold on to your chest voice as you move up your range, your voice will tighten up and you won't reach those higher notes. Often, singers are holding on to their chest resonance to maintain the power in their sound. This is a dead end. We will find all the power you need through a different, healthier method, later on.

If you want to hear someone moving up and down their mix without any chest tension, listen to Audra MacDonald's recording of "Your Daddy's Son" from the Original Broadway Cast Recording of *Ragtime*.

Placement

Placement is one of the most important concepts in singing. It's also much debated.[iii] Placement can mean different things to different people, while some people don't believe in placement at all. Part of this divide is, again, down to the different perspectives of sensation and science. Placement is an old idea that comes from the sensations singers experience. Here's Jerome Hines explaining it in *The Four Voices of Man*[7]:

> *"Placement" is commonly associated with very real feelings of vibration in different parts of the chest, throat and head, particularly in what is referred to as the "mask"... Most women described the mask as that region around and behind the eyeballs including the sinuses and the nasal passages. Some men include the dome of the hard palate and the upper teeth when speaking of the mask.*

This vibratory sensation has led to singers being told to direct the sound high and forward into the face in order to "place" the voice. The concept of directing the sound is what the scientific perspective takes issue with. Here's Stephen Smith in *The Naked Voice*[8]:

> *We seem to be able to make resonance happen in a specific place and are therefore lulled into thinking that it is active rather than passive. This concept is often referred to as* placement, *meaning we are putting resonance in a specific place. However, the nature of resonance is passive response and can't really be placed anywhere.*

A team of researchers in Estonia investigated placement, in 2002.[9] They agreed that the human body cannot literally direct sound into a particular space, like the chest or face; however, the concept of placement is a valid one in learning to sing. They write that placement "seems to have a meaning that – within certain limits – can be objectively defined, and that is understood similarly by students and professors." They also showed that from the third of our perspectives – that of sound – there is a difference in voices that are well placed. Placement boosted the overtones of the voice, increasing its richness and sonority.

But there is some validity to placement from the scientific perspective, as well. It isn't linked to the mechanics of sound but rather the

---

iii Like breathing. And support. And registers. I'm beginning to think no-one in singing agrees on anything.

anatomy of the voice. Part of the point of whole-body singing is to create the conditions for the larynx to function at its best. We've explored the larynx and the web of muscles that supports it like a sling. There are some big muscles in that web that we can directly, consciously control but there are also several muscles, often linked to making sound, which we can't. Dr Ted Dimon says these muscles "come into play in response to our intention to make sound or to communicate."[10] He goes on to explain that placement is the way to mobilise these muscles to help you make your best sound:

> The only way we can influence them is by thinking of the resultant sound or quality they seem to produce, heard usually as a form of vibration that centres on a particular part of the body. By experimenting with these different forms of vibration and resonance – all of which we try to get by asking the student to "direct" the sound in a particular location associated with a particular kind of vibration – the singer is able to influence and, eventually, to gain control over these functions – what we call placing the voice.

So, if you choose to work with placement, it can guide you to the right sensations for good singing and it can awaken muscles in your larynx which will help to keep your singing healthy and lead you to more advanced techniques such as belting.

When I teach placement, I tell students there are two vital elements to it: it has to be high and it has to be forward. The sensation you are looking for is a vibrant buzzing somewhere between your eyebrows. As this builds, it can spread across the top half of the face, like a superhero mask of resonance. Note that this is not nasality: you should avoid the sensation of buzzing in your nose and, instead, aim for the high, forward sensation between your eyebrows. When you feel this all the time, on all vowels, all pitches, all dynamics, then your voice is placed. Again, the guidance of a teacher is invaluable.

Developing placement is the same as building a muscle, it needs daily exercise and, in time, it will grow; so let's start with the best exercise for placement: humming. Humming makes it easier to focus your sound into the high, forward position. Remembering your whole-body engagement from Chapters 1 and 2, you're going to hum a small scale, slide, or phrase, quite low in your mix, and then repeat it moving a step higher each time. You want to cover about this much of the keyboard, shown in Figure 3.3.

When you hum, you have three choices of sound. The usual hum is an "m" sound. You can also use "n" with the tip of the tongue on the inside ridge above your top teeth. Or you can use "ng", like you have

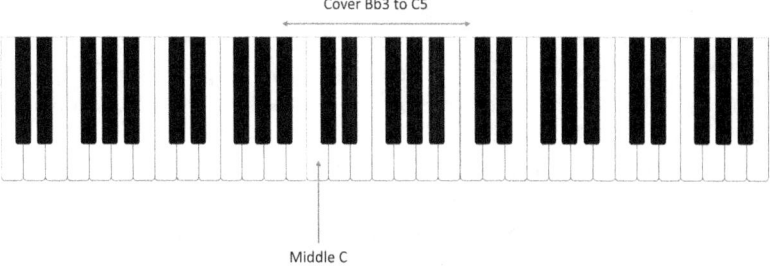

Figure 3.3 An approximate range for beginning resonance exercises.

just said the word "ring" or "sing". One of those sounds is usually best for opening up your placement so experiment to find which is the one for you. If you are still struggling to find the buzz, imagine the sound is very forward, even out in the space in front of you. You can also try tilting your head forward and down, bringing your chin closer to your chest. This position often helps singers find more buzz. Just be careful to keep the back of the neck long and do not squash your throat. You may also find it easier to start higher and descend in pitch. Your head placement is often more easily linked to your head voice, so it can make sense to start in that register. Do whatever works.

Once you have found the buzzing vibrancy on a hum, open up the sound to a vowel. I like this exercise, shown in Figure 3.4.

Here, you start on the hum and move seamlessly to the vowel. There are five vowels to practice: ee, eh, ah, oh, and ooh; as in the words tree, fair, car, hot, and who, pronounced in standard British English. Monitor your sensation of vibrancy as you do this exercise. Many singers encounter some difficulty maintaining the buzzy feeling when they change from a hum to a vowel. Often, the closed vowels "ee" and "oo" work best so start with those. "Ah" is an open vowel and can be the trickiest one for finding the buzz. Make sure your tongue is

Figure 3.4 An exercise to increase the feeling of resonance and placement. Start by humming then open up to a vowel while maintaining the same feeling of resonance.

still touching your bottom teeth, your soft palate remains high, and you have plenty of space between your back teeth. Moving to a vowel can cause some of that space to collapse. Overrule any such impulse. Maintain the space and direct the sound into the high, forward placement between your eyebrows.

Placement demands the use of your facial muscles. Your cheeks and eyes have to enliven and tone up. Think bright, lifted, and positive. Avoid getting the eyebrows involved, if possible. This lifted feeling helps the sound get up into your head. As we explored earlier, it is also activating lots of support muscles around your larynx that otherwise would not have switched on. This is vital for the healthy and expressive working of your voice. Watch singers like Kristin Chenoweth and Audra MacDonald and you will see the tone in their facial muscles as they perform. It's not just the face, though. Remember, the chain of support goes all the way to the floor. Your facial muscles are supporting your placement. And the lift in your rib cage is supporting your facial muscles. And the strength in your legs is supporting your rib cage. And the ground is supporting your legs and feet. Whole-body singing, all the time.

Two types of resonance

To build a complete picture of singing, we need to differentiate between two types of resonance: (1) the resonance you feel and (2) the resonance you produce. This is another split between the perspectives of sensation on one side and science and sound on the other. So far, in talking about placement, we've focused on the resonance you feel – the high, forward, buzzy feeling between your eyebrows. That sensation is an excellent guide to you the singer that your voice is working as it should and we will come back to it again and again. But it's worth knowing about the resonance that occurs inside you which enriches the sound of your singing.

The scientific perspective tells us that resonance is the amplification and enrichment of a sound. It happens when a soundwave bounces around in a space becoming stronger and fuller. Resonance is the reason you sound better singing in your bathroom than your living room because the hard surfaces of the bathroom bounce the sound around whereas the soft furnishings of the lounge swallow it up. When your vocal folds come together and vibrate, they don't create your full sound. The vibrations bounce around in your vocal tract creating resonance. From the sound perspective, this is the resonance your audience can hear. They cannot hear the resonant feeling you experience in your head.

Your vocal tract is the tunnel of space from your vocal folds up the rest of your throat and out of your nose and mouth. It contains your primary resonators. These are the ones bouncing the sound around, making it stronger and richer. Your primary resonators are your pharynx, mouth, and nasal cavities. To be clear on your pharynx, that is the space in your throat, just above the larynx. To get an idea of its location, put a hand on the back of your head and find the bone that sticks out at the bottom of your skull (the external occipital protuberance). Just below that is a soft, spongy area. That's your pharynx. If you put a finger on that and draw it around your face in a straight line, you should reach your mouth.

If the soft tissue in your vocal tract is toned up (making it more bathroom, less lounge), the sound will resonate and you will sound better. You can control this directly and indirectly, as Dr Ted Dimon pointed out in the quote on page 29. To take direct control of toning up your vocal tract, you can do three things:

1 You can lift the soft palate. The soft palate is at the back of your mouth. If you touch your tongue to the back of your top teeth, then run it backwards over the roof of your mouth, you will feel a change from the hard roof to the soft palate. The soft palate is made of muscle and tissue which can go up and down. If you lift the soft palate, you create a bigger, more toned up resonant space for your voice. That's why you were probably taught to do it as a child.

2 The tip of the tongue should touch the back of the bottom teeth. If it doesn't, it's in danger of slipping back and clogging up the resonant space in your throat.

3 Open the space between your back teeth. We can do a simple exercise for this; just make sure you've got clean hands. Put your little fingers into your mouth and get the tips of those fingers between your very back teeth. Now open that space between the back teeth. Keep doing that, keep your tongue on your bottom teeth, lift your soft palate, and breathe through your mouth: you should feel cool air at the back of your throat. That cool air feeling is a useful indicator that your primary resonators are open and toned up. It's important you maintain that feeling as you sing.

Indirect control of your primary resonators is achieved through placement, as we have seen. Putting the sound high and forward activates the facial muscles which activate lots of supporting muscles in the larynx.

Breathing with placement can engage both direct and indirect control of your primary resonators. To take a placed breath, imagine that the air doesn't only travel down into your lungs, it travels up into the high, forward space in your head. (This is sometimes likened to the feeling of preparing to bite into an apple.) You open a space like a bell for the sound to resonate, while also keeping the soft palate up, tongue forward, and back teeth open. Then when you sing, the air flows up through your open vocal tract and strikes that bell, and the sound comes from your high, forward placement. This will give you a richer sound and it will engage your voice in a healthier, more efficient manner. You will sound better and sing better.

A final point on this is that, unlike instruments, we produce sounds with words and those words can distort the shape of the vocal tract and our primary resonators. Part of learning to sing is maintaining the same resonant space with whatever words you are singing.

Head voice some of the time; head placement all of the time

Let's continue building your sense of placement. You must make a clear distinction between head voice and head placement. Head voice is a register and sometimes you sing up there and sometimes you don't. Head placement is a sensation that should be vibrating all the time, on every note, whichever register you are in. This is the key to moving smoothly through your registers.

Try performing a siren from very high to very low. This is different to the earlier, "breathy" siren we used to get the air flowing. This siren should be performed in full voice. Start with the high, forward placement you've been developing. As you go down from your head voice to your mix, the goal is to maintain the buzzy feeling in your head and allow it to spread to a buzzy feeling in your chest, too. When you siren from very low to very high, the reverse happens: you start with a buzzy feeling in your head and your chest, then as you get higher, the chest resonance is released and you are left with only the head resonance. If you ever find yourself low in your voice with chest placement only, it's going to be near impossible to move smoothly and comfortably up your range – this is just as true in songs as it is in exercises. So, when your voice moves, it should be pinned to your head placement, spread down to your chest, and return to your head as required, like a yo-yo tied to your head placement but dropping down and up, down and up.

By maintaining your high, forward placement, you will also find the real power in your voice. Remember that we mentioned some singers try to maintain their power by chesting through their range? Well, that does not work and it certainly is not sustainable over years of performing. Healthy power in singing comes from the forward part of the high, forward placement. As you go up through your mix, the head placement spreads across your eyes, becoming more forward, like a superhero mask of resonance. You can feel your muscles opening into it. That forward resonance makes the sound cut down a theatre – that's why placement is also referred to as "blade". So, you get your power from a quality in the resonance of your sound, not the volume of your sound.

Belting

Belting has become one of the defining sounds in Musical Theatre. When it's done well, it's thrilling. It should also be easy and healthy. But pinning down a definition of belting is difficult. To do that, we can turn again to our three perspectives of sensation, sound, and science.

Belting is considered to have started in the early part of the 20th century. Singers had to walk on to the stage with no microphones and still be heard at the back of the theatre. Opera singers had been doing that for a couple of hundred years or so but they did it by sticking to their head voice. Musical Theatre singers – possibly because of a desire to deliver text rather than music – kept a more speech-like quality to their sound which meant adding more chest. Chest plus head equals mix. Belting is a mix. It happens in your mix register. We will see this confirmed by numerous singers, teachers, and students, shortly.

Here is the first important difference between the sound and the sensation. Listeners hear belt as a "chesty" sound. But as a performer, if you aim to put chest into your belt it will almost certainly ruin you. We will find the right mixture (i.e., the right balance of head and chest) indirectly. It's important to remember this when working with professionals, too. A musical director may ask you for a particular sound, something "chestier", "more speechy", or "brassier". They don't know the intricacies of your singing technique because that's not their job. Their job is to get the best sound for the production. It's your job to deliver it and that means knowing how to deliver the sound they want via a technique that's healthy for you.

Who's belting and who's not?

One of the earliest belters is Ethel Merman. You can hear her sustaining a belted C5 in a recording of "I Got Rhythm" from Gershwin's *Girl, Crazy*, made in 1930. In those days, C5 was considered the top of the belt range, and it stayed that way for decades. It was only recently with the influence of pop/rock singing, and musicals such as *Wicked* (2003), *Chaplin: The Musical* (2006), *The Pirate Queen* (2006), and *Wonderland* (2009), that the belt range extended higher to F5.

So, we can agree that belting happens over the approximate range C4-F5. But it's certainly not the case that every time those notes appear in a song, the singer is belting them. Think of a song such as "Part of Your World" from *The Little Mermaid*. Jodi Benson's recording from the original Disney film goes from C4-C5. It's all mixed but it is not belted. Therefore, let's distinguish between mix-belt (like Ethel Merman "I Got Rhythm") and mix-sung (like Jodi Benson "Part of Your World"). To get a crystal clear demonstration of the difference between these two, compare the versions of "Defying Gravity" from *Wicked* by Idina Menzel and Lea Salonga. Idina Menzel's Originial Broadway Cast Recording is a paradigm of mix-belt. But Lea Salonga's version (available at https://www.youtube.com/watch?v=ImJ9YlftkEs) is mix-sung.

Below are some further examples. This aural distinction is a matter of judgement, not science, and so there won't be absolute agreement on whether a sound is mixed or belted but there should be enough of a consensus to guide our work in performance.

Mix-sung:

- Paige O'Hara – "Belle" – *Beauty and the Beast* Original Disney Soundtrack
- Audra MacDonald – "Flora the Red Menace: Sing Happy" – from the album *Sing Happy*
- Stephanie J. Block – "Woman" – *the Pirate Queen* Original Broadway Cast recording
- Sutton Foster – Gimme, Gimme, Gimme – *Thoroughly Modern Millie* Original Broadway Cast Recording
- Barbara Streisand – "Don't Rain on My Parade" – *Funny Girl* The Original Soundtrack Recording
- Liza Minelli – Maybe This Time – *Cabaret* 1972 film

Mix-belt:

- Idina Menzel – Defying Gravity – *Wicked* Original Broadway Cast Recording
- Jenn Collela – All Falls Down – *Chaplin: The Musical* Original Broadway Cast Recording
- Cynthia Erivo – I'm Here – *The Colour Purple* New Broadway Cast Recording

- Kara Lindsay – Watch What Happens – *Newsies* Original Broadway Cast Recording
- Leslie Grace – Breathe – *In The Heights* – Original Motion Picture Soundtrack

The science behind belting

Now let's consider the science. Scientific research into belting is in its early days. More studies are being done but many questions remain. The most important question for us is how do we take what the science is telling us and turn it into something useful for learning to sing. Let's start with the building blocks of the physicality of singing: breath, vocal folds, and larynx.

In 2015, scientists in Sweden published a study comparing belt and non-belt professional singing.[11] They found there was no specific breathing technique for belting. Different singers belted with different breathing techniques. They also found that individual singers did not change their breathing when they moved between belt and non-belt: "This speaks against the conclusion that belt needs to be produced with a specific type of breathing strategy." Therefore, do not change the set-up we have outlined for breathing when it comes to belting. Do the same as you usually do.

There are several components to consider in the working of the vocal folds. These include: those thick and thin muscles we mentioned earlier, the thyroarytenoid and the cricothyroid; the air pressure below the vocal folds that builds up to get them working; and how much the vocal folds are meeting as you produce a sound. Researchers agree that belting uses more of the thick TA muscle than the thinner CT muscle.[12] That's why you sometimes hear belting referred to as a "thick fold sound". The vocal folds also spend more time in contact together (the technical term is adducted, meaning "bring together"; the opposite is abducted, as in taken away). A piece of joint research between Stockholm and New York in 1993 found the air pressure below the vocal folds – known as sub-glottal pressure – is higher for belting than in mixed (i.e., mix-sung) or classical singing.[13] These findings were confirmed in the 2015 Swedish study that looked at breathing, above. In classical singing, the larynx is dropped low. But a study in the Netherlands in 1993 has shown it is higher in belting.[14] This was also the finding of the team from Stockholm and New York. They added that the pharynx was more constricted than in classical or mixed singing, as was part of the larynx.[15]

How does this bit of the science help you as a singer? Unfortunately, when it comes to belting, it might do you more harm than good. Look at the paragraph above. It states that belting uses a high, narrow larynx with a constricted pharynx. Can you imagine trying to apply that to your throat? It would feel horrible and you'd lose your voice in a week. Similarly, if you think of "thick fold mode" for your belt, you will just end up trying to chest too high with equally catastrophic results. Scientific instruments measure things as absolutes; our bodies sense things as relative. When you were a child, you might have taken part in the following science experiment. There are three bowls of water: one hot, one cold, and one medium. You put one hand in the hot bowl and the other hand in the cold bowl and leave them there for a while. Then you put both hands into the medium bowl. Even though the water is a single temperature (absolute), your hands feel it as cold or hot depending on which bowl they were in before (relative). So, if we say belting has a high larynx, exactly how high for you the singer depends on your larynx, where you normally place it during singing, and how much you need to adjust it for belting. Therefore, to successfully create the belt sound yourself, you must prioritise sensation.

Belting for you, the singer

Among the young women I have taught to belt successfully, the sensations that accompany belting are remarkably similar. They all describe:

- an intense feeling of energy in the body, often compared to standing on the edge of a tall cliff looking down at the sea
- a whole-body engagement
- a very high, forward placement
- no feeling of chest voice
- use of a heady mix
- an easy, safe production

But don't take my word for it! In 2019, singer and teacher Dr Christianne Roll published a study in which she talked to 17 female students and professionals, studying with master teachers in New York, about the best way to belt.[16] In this article, the singers give clear descriptions of the sensations they experience and the techniques they employ when belting. I have summarised the students' views, in Table 3.2.

This framework for belting is becoming increasingly secure. Writing in the *Journal of Singing*, a trio of singers, teachers, and researchers stated the importance of placement to accessing belt: "Teachers should

Table 3.2 Descriptions of the sensations and techniques of belting

Sensation or Technique	Text from Dr Roll's study
Whole-Body Engagement	"The singers in this study compared belting to a full-body workout, where every part of their body needs to be engaged to produce the sound correctly." "…all singers in this study credited bodily support, specifically engaging the abdominal muscles, as a necessary component for belt vocal exercises. This support from the body while singing higher and sustained belt notes protected the singers from the uncomfortable feeling of tension and, as Singer 12 called it, 'grabbing' in their throats."
Use of mix register for belting, rather than chest	"When specifically asked if the use of their mix-belt voice played into the production of the higher belt range, fifteen singers responded yes." [The other two didn't answer the question.] "The singers discussed their struggle with using too much chest register when belting, which can limit belt range and cause tension and believe their teacher's exercises are key to helping them find a lighter approach. This lighter approach is critical to their success as belters for vocal health, longevity, and producing higher belt notes." "Mix-belting seems to have emerged as a new type of belting technique to produce the higher range of belting in an easier way." "According to Singer 2, 'The notes that are in that high, high belt are in a mix. Mixing and belting are pretty synonymous. If it's in full chest, the audience is going to worry about the singer.'" "Belting is not perceived as a pure chest voice function. Every female belter in this study was observed to have easy access to her head voice."
Sensation of high, forward placement	"…another group of six singers…mentioned the need for a more forward and pointed resonance for producing notes in the high belt range." "Whether sung or spoken, the singers preferred belt exercises that encourage a forward resonance. Many belt exercises discussed by the singers, and observed in voice lessons, used bright syllables such as [njæ] and [wei]. The singers felt that these exercises help them get into a 'correct place' for belting."

encourage students to develop bright and forward resonance qualities for belt and mix".[17] Meanwhile, Professor Andrew White, from the University of Nebraska, emphasises the *relative* height of the larynx: "The position of the larynx in belt is more neutral (not elevated, as some contend)", and he emphasises the importance of keeping head voice in the mix for belting: "...belters benefit from the study of classical technique. 'TAD' means exactly that: 'thyro-arytenoid-*dominant*.' Belting should never be TA exclusively. Working the CT muscle like a classical soprano is an important component of any belter's vocal regimen".[18] And Singer and Professor Norman Spivey has surveyed a considerable amount of research on belting.[19] He found that, when it came to support for belting, "The whole body is working harder... [the] amount of energy is immense...[there is] greater muscular support from the body."

A few years before the results of what the students said in Dr Roll's study, the author published the views of the four top-level teachers in New York on belting and how to achieve it.[20] The teachers were unanimous in encouraging the use of head voice in every lesson on belting while reducing the amount of chest voice. Their students all worked their entire vocal range; sang with lots of physical energy; sang with bright, forward vowels; and sang in their mix for belting. Further, the teachers again and again returned to the importance of placement.

- "Veronica's[iv] exercises focused on resonance strategies to find a high, forward 'pocket' of resonance...To sing the more contemporary belt songs, which often extended into the range of C5 to F5, her women simply continued to negotiate the balance of registration and place the sound into the highest 'pocket' of resonance."
- "For higher belt notes, [Veronica's] students discussed the need for very high resonance, more head voice, and letting go of a lot of chest voice weight while still maintaining a thread of connection to it."
- "For higher belt notes, [Charles's] students discussed the need for a higher placement, more physical energy, modified vowels, less vibrato, and fighting the urge to flip to a legit, lofty sound."
- "...Gregory's students focused on the direction and placement of the sound, and trying to feel pressure in their face, not the throat."

The work we have done from the beginning of this book has prepared you for the physical set-up necessary for belting. We've established

---

iv The teachers who took part in the research were given pseudonyms, as is customary in academic studies.

a whole-body engagement which is fully energised and toned; we've encouraged a high, forward placement, all the time; and we've worked your mixed voice to its fullest. That set-up stays the same whether you are belting, singing legit, or mix-singing. What changes to get you to belting is your intention and action through that set-up.

As a reminder, the common factor in mix-belt and mix-sung is the mix. So, the foundation for both techniques requires an ability to move up through your mix as high as F5. This is where you will be rewarded by all the work on posture and placement. Remember, your posture must be alive, energised, and toned. It is not relaxed. It has a dynamic tension, rather than a static tension. It is closer to the energy you feel in the silence before you begin a dance routine. The body breathes and opens, enlivening the muscles and opening the placement space in your head. You lead with head placement all the time. As you sing in your mix and get higher, any chest placement drops away. Your head placement is the crown of your stack of support that starts with the ground beneath your feet. You spend the air, running it through your body like fuel through an engine. If you do all this, and you intend to communicate, you will make a very fine mix-sung sound.

To get from mix-sung to mix-belt, you create exactly the same set-up but you change your intention from singing to speaking. This is not everyday speaking. This is speaking on a high pitch, through the placement spot in your head. This links very well with two of the images from the New York master teachers. Firstly, the "pocket of resonance". This is what we are going to find by speaking into that high, forward placement. Secondly, the "thread of connection" to your chest. Just by intending to speak, you create that thread. You need nothing more from your chest voice. The intention will create the connection. Remember what we learned earlier from Dr Ted Dimon: the muscles in the larynx "come into play in response to our intention to make sound or to communicate."[21] The New York students mentioned above were committed to the "speaking" intention in belting:

> *For eight singers, connecting speech to singing is an integral part of their belt voice work. When the singers are struggling with belting a phrase, they recall their teacher's suggestion of "just say this sentence," and find that they have better success with belting...For another group of six singers, belting is produced by linking the sound to speech, regardless of pitch. According to Singer 15, 'When I do it, I just feel where I would say it in that range and that's where I put it.'*[22]

Try the following exercise. Stand with your posture highly energised. Remember to connect from the floor all the way up. Your breath runs through the system in the same way as the rest of your singing. Do a preparatory sigh to feel that sense of flowing air. Your placement is even further forward. Imagine that superhero mask spread that I mentioned earlier. Now, sing the following five-note scale in your mix on an "ee" vowel, as shown in Figure 3.5.

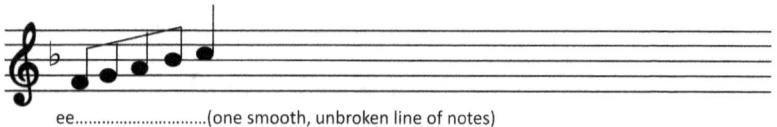

ee............................(one smooth, unbroken line of notes)

Figure 3.5 A scale performed in mix-sung.

That's mix-sung. Now try it again but instead of singing, imagine speaking the "ee" vowel on pitch through that placement space ("pocket of resonance") in your head, as shown in Figure 3.6.

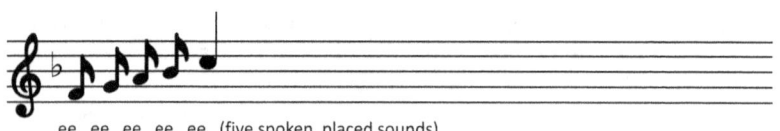

ee...ee...ee...ee...ee...(five spoken, placed sounds)

Figure 3.6 The same scale but performed in mix-belt.

The first, mix-sung scale from F4 to C5 should feel smooth, easy, with lots of breath moving through the body.

In the second, mix-belt scale, each note is separated and rings through the placement spot in your head. Each note should feel "spoken".

Once you can feel the difference between these two modes of singing, you can raise the pitch of the exercises and head towards F5. Do not rush to get there! I always tell my students, "you don't get high notes by practising high notes." That way of practising is ruinous. You have to develop your whole-body conditions plus your placement, day by day, and then the high notes will come.

When you feel ready, experiment with phrases from songs. For example, take the first chorus from "In My Dreams" from *Anastasia*. This is strong mix-belt territory, especially the notes from G4-C5. Sing it through with whole-body engagement and high, forward placement with an easy mix-sung sound. Then change it up and instead of "singing", speak the words through your high, forward placement. Beware that by speaking you do not immediately put the sound on your throat. Keep it high and bright. Notice the similarities in your set-up and the differences in your intention and action. That's the key.

Tuning

Hitting the right notes is a prerequisite of good singing. As Dr Ingo Titze wrote, "A singer is simply expected to be in tune with the prescribed melody."[23] If we're struggling to hit the right note in a song, it might be an aural issue or it might be a physical issue.

The best way to improve your aural tuning is to join a choir. Being surrounded by other voices and tuning your notes to theirs in unison as well as harmony, trains your ear in a way nothing else can. It's like learning French: you can study with apps and books and classes, but you're better off spending the summer in Paris.

When you sing in any ensemble, be that a choir or a chorus in a show, you can develop a feeling for notes as they relate to other notes. This is different to singing solo where it is possible (though not preferable) to feel the melody in isolation. Notes related to other notes is the fundamental concept of tuning. You can try this at the piano. Pick a note and, starting there, sing a simple five-note scale up and down. Then sing the scale again but this time hold the note down. Notice how every note you sing should tune to the first note of the scale.

Your physical engagement plays a big role in your tuning (see the concept map in the Introduction). Sometime singers go flat or sharp because their physicality is wrongly engaged rather than for lack of aural ability. For example, if your body has dropped during a phrase, a subsequent high note might come out flat because the body is no longer at the engagement level necessary to support the sound. The same thing happens with placement. If you don't maintain the high, forward feeling of resonance, you can get stuck with too much chest register meaning high notes are again slightly under pitch. The opposite is rarer but can happen. Singers can get so focused on their high, forward placement, they forget the connection to the body and the sound becomes so bright it goes sharp. To remedy this, simply re-connect to your whole-body engagement, all the way to the floor.

As you increase your awareness of placement, you can create an even finer level of tuning which brings a sweetness to your sound. Fine tuning is the result of your overtones (sometimes called harmonics), the frequencies of sound your voice produces above the main frequency of the note. They are the reason your voice sounds like your voice and not like a violin or a flute, even though you all could be producing the same fundamental tone. You produce the right overtones through your high, forward placement and, as you experiment with this, you should find that sweetness in your tuning. This is sometimes called "being on the shiny side of the note". If you sing with no placement, you'll hear a darker, more matt tuning.

A tuning issue common to Musical Theatre surrounds the qualities of vibrato and straight tone. It is a stylistic characteristic of Musical Theatre that long notes have a substantial period of straight tone before the vibrato comes in. Sometimes, the straight tone portion can sound flat, with the note only finding its true pitch with the vibrato. There are two possible reasons for this. Firstly, a study carried out by the Universities of Southampton and York discovered that it is indeed harder to tune straight tone notes. The oscillation (waving of pitch) of vibrato gives a greater range of "being in tune" than straight tone.[24] Secondly, I have found that singers sometimes exert a small grip on their throat to prevent vibrato coming in. This gripping stops the larynx working at its most efficient and so this too could have the effect of pulling a note flat. When that gripping is relaxed, allowing vibrato, the larynx can function efficiently again and the note turns true.

Whistle tones

Before we conclude this chapter on voice, let's take a moment to meet the mysterious "whistle tones". These are also known as whistle register, flute register, and flageolet register. This phenomenon has received limited attention from professionals and academics but it is worth clarifying. If you remember our discussion on registers, there was the classification method M0, M1, M2, and M3. M0 is vocal fry; M1 is chest voice; M2 is head voice; and M3 is whistle tones. A French research team studied the larynx using electronic scans to observe what happens in trained and untrained singers.[25] They found the whistle tones are "the highest-pitched sounds of the human voice, but it is seldom used either in speech or in singing." They describe the physicality of whistle tones as having very thin, tightly stretched vocal folds and a small opening in the glottis. If you want to hear it in action, listen to Minnie Ripperton's recording of "Here We Go". At 2'30", you'll hear her sing the phrase "here we go" in whistle register.

Whistle tones are rarely employed in Musical Theatre. In popular song, they most often appear as decorations and displays of vocal fireworks. You can explore them but you are at little disadvantage if they are not in your technique.

Summing up

In this chapter, we have used sensation, sound, and science, to explore the workings of your voice. We have used a three-register system of placement: head, mix, and chest. We have also seen the prime importance of placement, in your singing. Make sure your placement is always high and forward. Combining placement and registers led us towards belting. All we needed to add was the intention to speak through your high, forward placement.

The final aspect of your physicality as a singer is maintaining vocal health. This is vital for your career and for your own sense of well-being. This is where we turn to in Chapter 4.

Notes

1 Marchesi, M. (1887) *Bel Canto: A Theoretical and Practical Vocal Method*. Enoch and Sons.
2 Kessler Price, K. (2011) "Emma Seiler: A Pioneering Woman in the Art and Science of Teaching Voice", *Journal of Singing*, 68:1, 12.
3 Hall, K. (2014) *So You Want to Sing Music Theatre*, p. 34; and Warwick, J. and Adrian, A. (editors) (2016) *Voicing Girlhood in Popular Music: Performance, Authority, Authenticity*, p. 101.
4 Roubeau, B., Henrich, N. and Castellengo, M. (2009) "Laryngeal Vibratory Mechanisms: The Notion of Vocal Register Revisited", *Journal of Voice*, 23:4, 437, Table 5.
5 Marchesi, M. (1887) "Practical Guide for Students: Registers of the Female Voice".
6 Smith, W.S. (2007) *The Naked Voice: A Wholistic Approach to Singing*, OUP, p. 18.
7 Hines, J. (1997), p. 50.
8 Smith, W.S. (2007), pp. 16–17.
9 Vurma, A. and Ross, J. (2002) "Where Is a Singer's Voice If It Is Placed "Forward"?", *Journal of Voice*, 16:3, 383–391.
10 Dimon, T. (2011), p. 92.
11 Sundberg, J. and Thalén, M. (2015) "Respiratory and Acoustical Differences between Belt and Neutral Style of Singing", *Journal of Voice*, 29:4, 418–425.
12 Bourne, T., Garnier, M. and Kenny, D. (2011) "Music Theater Voice: Production, Physiology and Pedagogy", *Journal of Singing*, 67:4, 437–444, see especially p. 438.
13 Sundberg, J., Gramming, P. and Lovetri, J. (1993) "Comparisons of Pharynx, Source, Formant, and Pressure Characteristics in Operatic and Musical Theatre Singing", *Journal of Voice*, 7:4, 301–310.
14 Schutte, H.K. and Miller, D.G., (1993) "Belting and Pop, Nonclassical Approaches to the Female Middle Voice: Some Preliminary Considerations", *Journal of Voice*, 7:2, 142–150.
15 Sundberg, J., Gramming, P. and Lovetri, J. (1993), p. 306.
16 Roll, C. (2019) "The Female Broadway Belt Voice: The Singer's Perspective", *Journal of Singing*, 76:2, 155–162.
17 Bourne, T., Garnier, M. and Kenny, D. (2011) "Music Theater Voice: Production, Physiology and Pedagogy", *Journal of Singing*, 67:4, 441.
18 White, A. (2011) "Belting as an Academic Discipline", *American Music Teacher*, June/July, p. 23.

19 Spivey, N. (2008) "Music Theater Singing ... Let's Talk. Part 2: Examining the Debate on Belting", *Journal of Singing*, 64:5, 607–614.
20 Roll, C. (2016) "The Evolution of the Female Broadway Belt Voice: Implications for Teachers and Singers", *Journal of Voice*, 30:5, 639.e1–639.e9.
21 Dimon, T. (2011), p. 92.
22 Roll, C. (2019), pp.156 and 158.
23 Titze, I. (1988) "Control of Voice Fundamental Frequency", *Journal of Singing*, 45:2, 18.
24 van Besouw, R.M., Brereton, J.S. and Howard, D.M. (2008) "Range of Tuning for Tones with and without Vibrato", *Music Perception*, 26:2, 145–156.
25 Roubeau, B., Henrich, N. and Castellengo, M. (2009) "Laryngeal Vibratory Mechanisms: The Notion of Vocal Register Revisited", *Journal of Voice*, 23:4, 425–438.

4 Vocal Health

Singers have all sorts of routines, regimes, and superstitions for staying in good voice. Some never eat chocolate; some avoid tea and coffee; others drink honey and lemon or take a silent day of complete vocal rest; I was even warned about eating cake before a performance lest I was struck down with "cake throat". It's difficult to get definitive answers on what's best for the voice, partly because everybody's body is different (penicillin is a wonder drug but some people are allergic to it), but there are some facts we can separate from the fictions.

The very best thing for your voice is singing well. Developing a rock-solid technique as we have outlined in the first three chapters is what will sustain you through a career. Anything else, like drinking honey and lemon, is just an add-on to that. So the first thing to address, each day, is building that technique.

One of the worst things for singers is not singing but talking. When we sing, we sing on a solid technique. But we don't always talk on one. Breath and placement often go out the window. That means the effort is going into your vocal folds. If you spend the evening in a bar or restaurant and have to talk over a noisy room, you are in danger of straining your voice and you will likely feel the effects the next morning. The same thing could happen on a night in with family. Plan accordingly and don't get caught out in an audition or performance.

Hydration

Everyone knows water is good for singing, right? But how much water should you drink, when should you drink it, and what happens when you do? Water is an integral part of every system in the body so on a global level the better your body is working the better your voice is working. The reason water specifically helps the voice at a local level is that it helps create the mucus that lines the vocal folds, which, in turn, allows them to vibrate quickly and for long periods without getting sore. The traditional advice to maintain the right level of hydration is to drink until you pee pale.[1] But the science might not back this up. Dr Naomi Hartley and Professor Susan Thibeault at the University of Wisconsin reviewed several papers on the relationship between hydration and the voice.[2] They found that urine colour is not necessarily a reliable indicator of your overall body hydration. It's much more likely to suggest how much water you have just drunk: "…urine indices are more reflective of the recent volume of fluid intake than an accurate representation of overall hydration status." There is also no point drinking loads of water before you need to sing because your body will pee it out before the water has a chance to reach your body's systems, even if you are lacking in hydration: "The ingestion of a large volume of water has been shown to result in the excretion of diluted urine by the kidneys even when the body has an overall water deficit." If you are adequately hydrated, there is no clear indication that drinking more water will increase your performance level.

One of the common pieces of advice given to singers is to avoid substances that dehydrate you. That includes coffee, tea, alcohol, and particular medications like aspirin and decongestants. Some of these are said to "dry you out" either because they reduce the body's natural secretion or they are diuretics, that is, they make you pee. Again, Hartley and Thibeault suggest this is a myth: "examination of the literature reveals little evidence that such substances do indeed result in vocal change." There are at least two studies on the effect of drinking caffeinated coffee and they showed no detrimental effects on the voices of the participants. Another study looked at the effects of an antihistamine and a diuretic. They found no clear link to how well the voice worked. They concluded that "the respiratory system may retain fluids longer than other regions of the body during dehydration." At most, participants in one of these studies complained of a "dry throat" but there was no noticeable difference in their voices.

It appears to be better to think of hydration as a process over days rather than hours. Trying to rehydrate yourself at the last minute just doesn't work. It's also worth remembering that, as important as drinking water is, it only accounts for around 60% of your hydration needs; 30% comes from your food intake. So what you eat is vital to maintaining good hydration.[i] Despite the need to create a strong level of hydration,

---

i After 60% fluids and 30% food, the remaining 10% of your hydration needs comes from a process called catabolism. That's one of the two branches of your metabolism and it breaks down bigger molecules into smaller ones, releasing energy.

the research suggests that many people are not drinking enough water and it could have major impacts. "Deficits in hydration levels of as little as 1–2% have been shown to have detrimental effects on endurance, thermoregulatory capability, and motivation, and to increase fatigue and perceived effort. Heart rate is increased, muscle power is decreased, physiological strain is greater, and cognitive performance is reduced." It's clear that these would also cause problems in performance and you may find your vocals suffering because of an overall physical or mental tiredness. However, the research also suggests that our hydration states may be more robust than we give them credit for. If you create healthy hydration levels, having a coffee on the day of a performance is unlikely to trouble your voice.

While we're on the subject of food intake, let's be clear about the structure of your throat regarding air and food. The top of your throat divides into two pathways, one at the front and one at the back. The front one is the trachea or windpipe, which is for air and connects to the lungs. This is where your vocal folds are. The back one is the oesophagus, which is for food and connects to your stomach. When you swallow food, it does not touch your vocal folds. You cannot coat your vocal folds in chocolate or honey or cake or anything else that's destined for the stomach because it would choke you. Your hydration level is affected, as we have seen, by the process of food and fluid intake which is then digested and distributed around your body.

However, even though your vocal folds won't be directly affected by food and fluids, your throat can be. The word "throat" can encompass both the trachea (windpipe) and the oesophagus (food pipe). As soon as you eat, the food or fluid interacts with the lining of mucus from the mouth downwards. Drinking tea with honey and lemon feels good for your throat because it can coat the lining from the back of the mouth and down the oesophagus with a soothing film. That can give you a feeling of relief because it's in the general area of your throat; it just isn't in the specific area of your vocal folds. Conversely, if you eat something full of salt, like crisps or salted nuts, the salt can draw moisture out of that same mucus lining and suddenly your vocal mechanism may struggle to function. This has happened to me on stage. It was not pleasant.

The other problem connected with food that singers need to be aware of is reflux. Reflux is when the substances in your stomach, like acid and bile, escape and travel up your oesophagus causing things like heartburn. These substances can make it as far up as the larynx where they damage the mucus lining and can prevent it repairing itself.[3] Reflux can also leave your vocal folds more vulnerable to more serious problems like nodules. A review of the research into this area, carried out by a team in Belgium and France, found "singers are at high risk [of suffering reflux] because of necessary air support involving intense use of abdominal muscles, higher intra-abdominal pressure, increased stress due to career management and uncomfortable schedules, late meals just before sleep, bad nutrition habits like increased intake of citrus products, fatty foods and spicy foods."[4] Take note of those last few causes, from "late meals" onwards. They can be avoided and your voice, and your body, will thank you for it.

Let's return to hydrating your vocal folds because there is a way to get moisture directly onto your vocal folds: steaming. Steaming is becoming increasingly popular among singers. By inhaling steam, you can moisten the upper part of the vocal tract and the vocal folds. A 2020 study carried out in New York looked at the effect of steaming as a warm-up exercise for young women.[5] It also compared steaming with another increasingly popular exercise, blowing bubbles through a straw into a cup of water. The participants did three warm-ups: (1) steaming; (2) bubbles; and (3) steaming and bubbles consecutively. The results were mixed and the researchers found "No strategy was universally better than the others." However, they did note that when it came to vocal efficiency, steaming looked to be the most beneficial.

The participants did not steam for very long in this study, only three minutes, and they vocalised straight after. When I advise students to steam, I suggest 10–12 minutes followed by 20–30 minutes of silence or only light speaking. That seems to be a more effective regimen. There is also research that suggests adding a little salt to your steaming water is helpful. Researchers in the United States tested more than 30 sopranos using nebulisers with plain water or salt water.[6] They found the salt water was much more beneficial for vocal function.

To return to the blowing bubbles exercise, this is what is known as a Semi-Occluded Vowel Tract (SOVT) exercise. "Semi-Occluded" means partially closed so these are exercises where there is some measure of closure somewhere on the passage from your pharynx to your nose and mouth. When you did lip trills, "z", "v", and "rolled r" exercises earlier in the book, you were doing SOVT exercises. I have seen many conservatoire students going between lessons holding their bottles, blowing into their straws, and I question how much benefit they are getting. First of all, remember our golden rule for exercises: if you don't do them with whole-body conditions, they aren't worth much. The straw-in-bottle apparatus tends to make singers drop their heads down to reach the straw, ruining their singing posture. You would not lip trill in that position so why do any another SOVT exercise in that position? Second, the 2020 New York study reports this exercise can be dangerous if not done properly: "Even blowing bubbles into a cup of water with phonation can be done poorly, in some cases yielding counterproductive results." They go on to explain that there are a lot of variables that affect this exercise, including the length of your straw, its diameter, and how far it reaches into the water. The exercise was originated by a professor in Helsinki in the 1960s: "He determined the appropriate tube length for a client by palpating the larynx during phonation through the tube and feeling for the relationship between tube length and laryngeal lowering. In singers, his choice of tube length also corresponded to vocal category." He also put the straw (or tube) deeper into the water for singers who under-used their voices, and higher up for singers who overused their voices. Researchers in Sweden in 2013 studied the vocal effects of blowing through a straw for 12 mezzo-sopranos. They found the only singers who benefited were the ones who were not very experienced and did not practice daily. Singers who did got nothing from this exercise: "It seems likely that singers who practice daily reach an improved everyday phonatory condition that is not likely to be further improved with a short and simple exercise."[7] Adjustable, metal straws that are specially built for singers and do away with the bottle of water are now available to buy. I have no experience with these but some teachers have reported good results using them with students. My advice would be to consider the evidence above before investing!

One of the best things you can do for your voice is get a good night's sleep. World famous tenor, Luciano Pavarotti, said: "I sleep until eleven or twelve the day of the performance. I trust very much in rest for the voice."[8] More recently, a large survey was undertaken to prove the link between good sleep and good voice. In 2017, researchers in Brazil surveyed more than 800 people to confirm this link and they found that "a good night sleep is a fundamental factor for an adequate voice production."[9] They went on to explain why:

> *The lack of restorative sleep does not allow tissue recovery. Lack of tissue recovery, especially hydration, may influence vocal quality. During sleep, protein synthesis increases, repairing the damaged muscle fibers and building new tissues. Thus, sleep deprivation can influence the balance between protein synthesis and protein degradation, causing loss of muscle mass. Lower muscle mass in the vocal folds can lead to atrophy and arching, which may result in vocal deviation. Such modification can be perceived as breathiness caused by the increase of the passage of air between the arched vocal folds and/or roughness caused by the lack of vibrating mass.*[10]

The effect of the menstrual cycle on the voice

The effect of the menstrual cycle on the voice is something singers have known about for a long time, but researchers have only just begun to investigate. Women singing in opera houses across Europe used to have "grace days" written into their contracts when they would not be expected to sing. These days were usually the premenstrual days of their monthly cycle.[11] The kind of vocal problems women report include hoarseness, feeling vocally tired, decreased range especially at the very top, difficulties singing softly, lack of vibrato control, and difficulties pitching. This has all come under the label: Premenstrual Vocal Syndrome.

Several studies have now been conducted to try to understand what's happening. In 2017, a study of women who were not professional singers found their vocal folds became thicker during the premenstrual phase.[12] We should not be surprised that the larynx reacts to the release of sex hormones, that's what leads to a boy's voice breaking during puberty. What is more surprising is that scientists found a significant similarity between smear tests of the female vocal folds and the cervix. The lining of mucus in both behaves and reacts to hormones in the same way.[13] However, which hormones affect the female voice, and when they affect it, is still contested.

The traditional view has been that the effects on the voice are premenstrual, hence the name Premenstrual Vocal Syndrome. This is a stage at which water retention can occur, causing bloating. A 2017 review of the effects of menstruation on singing found that water retention "also leads to slight swelling or thickening of the vocal folds, which could impede the movements during the production of voice."[14] But it may not only be premenstrual. A 2009 Australian study of young singers at the Sydney Conservatorium of Music found there were also vocal effects midcycle, around ovulation: "the midcycle peak of hormones also apparently affects the voice detrimentally in association with body and mood states."[15] Further, these studies are usually focused on the female hormones oestrogen and progesterone, but a 2006 study on singers using the contraceptive pill suggested it's the male hormone testosterone that might be causing the problems.[16] "Testosterone and other androgenic [male] substances have adverse effects on the female singing voice, altering the length and extensibility of the connective tissue of the vocal folds and the vocal ligaments that allow the production of different registers during voice production." They go on to explain why women would be more affected by testosterone than men: "Women seem to be more susceptible to variations in laryngeal mucosa caused by testosterone than men despite the fact that concentrations of testosterone are much higher in men compared to women, because the percentage of cells that constitute the male laryngeal mucosa tend to remain constant through the whole month, whereas the cells of the female laryngeal mucosa change during the menstrual cycle." This study found testosterone was the hormone making the difference in how female singers felt about their voices. Other studies have noted the effect that testosterone has in women during the menopause.

It is also worth noting that irregular cycles can increase the effect on the voice. The Australian study mentioned earlier found "irregular menstrual cycles generally show more hormonal fluctuations and greater negative impact on the voice."[17] And, in addition to any hormone-induced vocal issues caused by the menstrual cycle, secondary effects can also be problematic. For example, if you suffer with stomach cramps, those are going to impact your ability to engage a low feeling of appoggio.

Not all women will find their voices affected by the menstrual cycle. One study records: "in an informal study of all female patients of child-bearing age not taking oral contraceptives, we noted that about 33% suffered from a vocal pre-menstrual syndrome."[18] However, it is possible that number is higher among singers because as a group we use our voices much more and so would be more likely to notice problems.

There is some more positive news amongst all this. The first is the effect of the contraceptive pill. Because it flattens out hormone levels, the voice can become more stable and reliable. The 2009 Australian study reports: "Results showed that those taking the oral contraceptive pill rated their voice quality higher than those not taking the pill...This supports [earlier] research... that the contraceptive pill has a stabilizing effect on the voice and may benefit female singers. The association of better mood with contraceptive pill use needs further exploration."[19]

The second piece of positive news is that when professional singer-teachers listened to recordings of the singers in that Australian study, they could not hear any deficiencies in their voices linked to where the singers were in their cycles. "Although singers were able to identify perceptually their singing samples taken at different times in their cycles, expert pedagogues did not reliably discern differences in vocal quality...Consequently, singers' education should include information that their perceptions regarding their vocal quality may not adversely affect perceptual quality."[20] In other words, you may know you're not singing at your best, but the audience or audition panel won't.

Marking

Once you are cast in a show, you are responsible for maintaining your vocal health. That includes managing yourself through the rehearsal process and into shows. One of the key techniques to preserving the health of your voice is "marking". In *On the Art of Singing*, Richard Miller describes marking as: "an international theatre term for the technique of sparing the voice during rehearsal. During marking, volume is reduced, high pitches may be lowered an octave, and very low pitches raised an octave."[21] I would add that high belt passages may be sung in your head voice to make them easier and without strain. You are not expected to sing out at full voice throughout an entire rehearsal, not to mention an entire rehearsal period. You are expected to manage your voice so that you can sing out fully for the dress rehearsal and opening night so pace yourself in the run up to those performances.

When you mark, maintain all the physical engagement you employ when singing full out. The danger of marking is that we sing quietly, drop the physical support, and end up putting more strain on the voice than if we had just sung out in the first place. Also, keep your text clear when you mark. Let the director and musical director see that you know what you're singing and when you should be singing it.

There's always a balance to marking. You want to sing out enough to get the part into your voice so don't mark all the time. Also, you'll have to work with your MD and other performers who may want to hear full singing at particular times. Generally, I find it's a good rule to sing out at the beginning of the rehearsal, and at the end of a rehearsal when you run all the work you've done that day. The bit in the middle when the focus is on something other than the music, like blocking or characterisation, can be an appropriate time to mark.

Illness

We are all human and we all get sick. The level of sickness is a scale. At one end is a level of sickness where you just cannot sing, either because you can't get out of bed or your vocal function is significantly impaired: migraine or flu would be examples of this. At the other end is a level of sickness where you can sing: a headache, for example, is unlikely to keep you in bed or stop your voice from working. The difficult decisions for us as performers lie in the area in between where maybe we could sing but maybe we shouldn't. Generally, this is going to be coughs and colds. The most significant element that makes a difference here is, once again, technique. Stephen Smith writes, "People with poor technique who get sick probably should cancel performances because they won't be able to cope with the illness. Those with a very good, strong, and healthy technique won't need to cancel as often because they are able to manage their voices despite unhealthy physical conditions." He goes on to add, "Generally, if singers are not running a fever or suffering from a serious vocal infection, they should be able to go on in a performance."[22] I find that the placement of the cough or cold is highly significant. As a general rule, if you feel it's on your throat (you might feel pain when you sing), then do not sing on it. If it's elsewhere, for example if you feel congested in your nose or face, then you could be ok. If singing when you are sick risks serious, irreversible damage – don't sing.

We should be cautious when combining singing with taking painkillers (analgesics) like aspirin and paracetamol. Pain is a warning sign. Writing in America's *Journal of Singing*, Professor Robert Thayer Sataloff warned of the dangers of blocking it out: "Pain is an important protective physiologic function. Masking it risks incurring significant vocal damage which may be unrecognized until after the analgesic or anaesthetic wears off."[23] You need to know if what you are doing is hurting your throat so check any medication, including throat lozenges, for analgesics.

Summing-up

We have outlined some clear dos and don'ts regarding vocal health. A solid place to start is to sing well, sleep well, and stay hydrated. Build yourself a solid technique and it will get you through, or at least mitigate, many of the other problems you will encounter. Beyond those, vocal health is often a matter of knowing your own body, what it reacts to, and how you can deal with it. This is an ongoing process, so be patient with yourself and trust your whole-body technique.

Notes

1. See, for example Hall, K. (2014) *So You Want to Sing Music Theatre: A Guide for Professionals*, Rowman and Littlefield, p. 43, and Smith, W.S. (2007) *The Naked Voice: A Wholistic Approach to Singing*, OUP, p. 165.
2. Hartley, N.A. and Thibeault, S.L. (2014) "Systemic Hydration: Relating Science to Clinical Practice in Vocal Health", *Journal of Voice*, 28:5, 652.e1–652.e20.
3. Lechien, J.R., Schindlerd, A., Robottie, C., Lejeunef, L. and Finck, C. (2019) "Laryngopharyngeal Reflux Disease in Singers: Pathophysiology, Clinical Findings and Perspectives of a New Patient-reported Outcome Instrument", *European Annals of Otorhinolaryngology, Head and Neck diseases*, 136, S39–S43.

4. Ibid., p. S41.
5. Keltz, A. and McHenry, M. (2020) "Steam and/or Semi Occluded Vowel Tract Exercise as Morning Vocal Warm-up Strategy", *Journal of Voice*, accepted for publication, https://doi.org/10.1016/j.jvoice.2020.08.037
6. Tanner, K., Roy, N., Merrill, R.M., Muntz, F., Houtz, D.R., Sauder, C., Elstad, M. and Wright-Costa, J. (2010) "Nebulized Isotonic Saline versus Water Following a Laryngeal Desiccation Challenge in Classically Trained Sopranos", *Journal of Speech, Language and Hearing Research*, 53, 1555–1566.
7. Enflo, L., Sundberg, J., Romedahl, C. and McAllister, A. (2013) "Effects on Vocal Fold Collision and Phonation Threshold Pressure of Resonance Tube Phonation with Tube End in Water", *Journal of Speech, Language and Hearing Research*, 56, 1530–1538, quote on p. 1534.
8. Hines, J. (1982) *Great Singers on Great Singing*, Limelight Editions, p. 217.
9. Rocha, B.R. and Behalu, M. (2017) "The Influence of Sleep Disorders on Voice Quality", *Journal of Voice*, 32:6, 771.e1–771.e13, quote on p. e7.
10. Ibid., p. e8.
11. Shoffel-Havakuk, H. et al. (2018) "Menstrual Cycle, Vocal Performance, and Laryngeal Vascular Appearance: An Observational Study on 17 Subjects", *Journal of Voice*, 32:2, 226, and Ryan, M. and Kenny, D.T. (2009) "Perceived Effects of the Menstrual Cycle on Young Female Singers in the Western Classical Tradition", *Journal of Voice*, 32:1, 99.
12. Shoffel-Havakuk, H. et al. (2018) "Menstrual Cycle, Vocal Performance, and Laryngeal Vascular Appearance: An Observational Study on 17 Subjects", *Journal of Voice*, 32:2, 226–233.
13. Abitbol, J., Abitbol, P. and Abitbol, B. (1999) "Sex Hormones and the Female Voice", *Journal of Voice*, 13:3, 435.
14. Gunjawate, D.R., Aithal, V.U., Ravi, R. and Venkatesh, B.T. (2017) "The Effects of Menstrual Cycle on Singing Voice: A Systematic Review", *Journal of Voice*, 31:2, 188.
15. Ryan, M. and Kenny, D.T. (2009) "Perceived Effects of the Menstrual Cycle on Young Female Singers in the Western Classical Tradition", *Journal of Voice*, 23:1, 107.
16. Lã, F.M.B, Ledger, W.L., Davidson, J.W., Howard, D.M. and Jones, G.L. (2007) "The Effects of a Third Generation Combined Oral Contraceptive Pill on the Classical Singing Voice", *Journal of Voice*, 21:6, 759.
17. Ryan and Kenny (2009), p. 100.
18. Abitbol et al. (1999), p. 438.
19. Ryan, M. and Kenny, D.T. (2009), p. 106. The "earlier research" is Comins J. "Scientists say pill could be good for your voice" [report on a research project]. *Singer*, 2002, 22–23 [Voice Clinic].
20. Ryan and Kenny (2009), p. 107–108.
21. Miller, R. (1996) *On the Art of Singing*, OUP, p. 165.
22. Smith, W.S. (2007) *The Naked Voice: A Wholistic Approach to Singing*, OUP, p. 174.
23. Sataloff, R.T. (1995) "Medications and Their Effects on the Voice", *Journal of Singing*, 52:1, 50.

Part II
Expressive Singing

5 Impression–Expression

In 1998, a gala concert was performed at London's Lyceum Theatre in honour of Cameron Mackintosh. It was called *Hey, Mr Producer* and, among the many star performances, one of the most memorable was Judi Dench's "Send In The Clowns" from *A Little Night Music*. For four and a half minutes, Judi Dench expressed the world of her character, with a depth of thought and feeling that drew rapturous applause from the audience. We're going to call this kind of performance "Expressive Singing" and Part II of this book is all about how to create it.

Your character inhabits a world which acts on her and she, in return, acts on it. This process is going on all the time and gives us the title of this chapter: "Impression" is the world making its mark on the character and "Expression" is the character doing something about it. We're going to explore the Impression, first, and this will begin to create the depth of engagement necessary to lead us to Expressive Singing. As the director Peter Brook wrote: "A word does not start as a word - it is an end product which begins as an impulse, stimulated by attitude and behaviour which dictates the need for expression."[1]

The Impression is something that happens in life that deeply impresses itself on the mind of the character. Consider a basic model of how you go through life. There is you, and outside of you, there is reality. Reality happens and you know about it through your five senses: sight, hearing, touch, taste, and smell. When something reaches you via your senses, like a sunset, a car horn, or a splash of cold water, it creates a readiness in you to react to it or do something about it.[i] When Mrs Lovett receives the Impression of the murdered Pirelli, she sees an opportunity to dispose of the body, get closer to Sweeney Todd, and boost her business at the pie shop. So, she takes action by beginning the duet "A Little Priest."

---

i Psychologists call this process "transduction".

DOI: 10.4324/9781003286875-8

The Impressions in the character's mind that stimulate action do not come from the world outside, only. We also have a world inside us of thoughts, feelings, memories, reasoning, and so on. These are equally capable of causing action. For example, when Fantine sings "I Dreamed a Dream", she's turning over memories of a lover and their time together. Often songs are a mix of both the external world and the character's internal world. Eponine in "On My Own" is caught between the internal fantasy of Marius taking a romantic walk with her and the external reality of the silent streets and the lonely river. Whichever kind of Impression it is, it's down to you as the performer to create the vividness of the Impression in your imagination that will trigger the Expression of the song.

When the character acts on her external or internal world, she receives more sensory feedback to assess how she's done – that means more Impressions. If we go back to Mrs Lovett with Todd and the dead Pirelli, her action is to tentatively sing the first line of the duet whereupon she waits to receive Todd's reaction before proceeding further. And so characters enter into a cycle of reality – sensation – action – reality – sensation – action; or as we can simplify it, Impression – Expression. Another of our great directors, Declan Donnellan, explained this cycle beautifully in his book *The Actor and the Target*. Starting with the Expression phase, he wrote: "To try to alter the other. To see it hasn't worked. To try something else. These three steps underpin all that an actor says and does."[2] When you perform a song, each phrase is an attempt to alter the other. Each phrase fails to do that and so you continue singing. If, for instance, after Mrs Lovett had begun her duet, Todd had instantly replied "You're right, we should use him as pie filling", then she would not need to sing any more. Your character has only ever altered things enough to stop singing by the end of the song.

This model of behaviour can be seen in the following diagram (Figure 5.1).

Within this model is one of the vital steps for reaching Expressive Singing: the Impression which motivates you to act is also the trigger for your whole-body engagement. In Part I, we outlined these processes mechanically, but now we see how they fit in as an integral part of Expressive Singing. The process goes like this. Because you are in a heightened emotional state where speech is no longer enough, you must sing. Deciding to sing is really a decision to try to alter your external or internal worlds. So when you breathe in, you do not breathe in to make a pretty sound or reach a high note, you breathe in on the feeling of what you want to express in order to change your world. As you do so, all the technical aspects of good singing kick in: your feet and legs

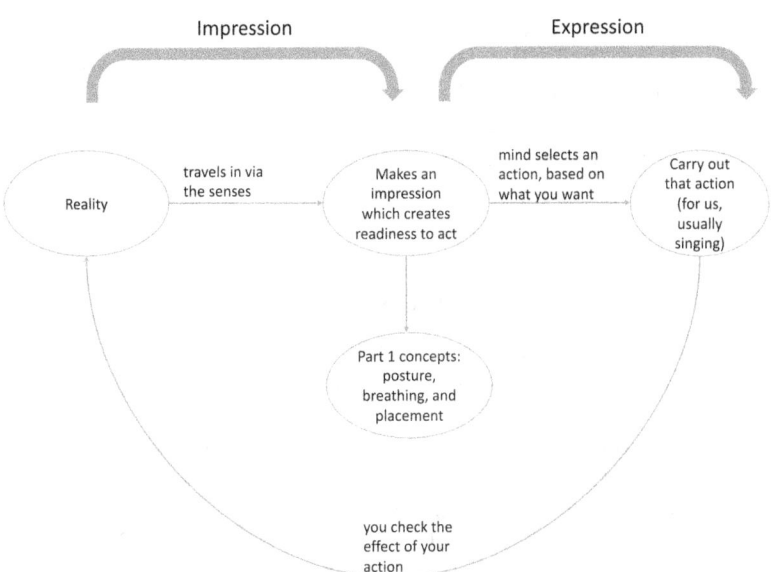

Figure 5.1 Impression–Expression. Your character is in a cycle of receiving Impressions and creating Expressions. This continues throughout a song, scene, act, and show.

connect to the ground, your pelvic floor engages, your rib cage lifts and opens, your face tones up, you create a resonant space for the sound, which includes every note in your range, and you open the placement space in your head to send the sound through. It's all a result of your inner demand to express something, which came about because of an Impression made on you.

Thomas Hemsley called the Impression the singer's "impulse". He wrote: "It is something much more basic, much more instinctive, more directly linked to 'the primaeval sounds and exclamations, with which men express their inner feelings and reactions to impressions from the world around them' (Manén, *Bel Canto*). This primitive impulse, together with a high degree of vital energy is the essential raw material of singing and must be cultivated and strengthened".[3] That means you have to build your imaginative engagement with the Impression in order for it to release the level of Expression demanded by Musical Theatre. We will look at exercises to achieve this, shortly.

Remember that your in-breath must be infused with the feeling you need to express. David F. Ostwald, in his book *Acting for Singers* wrote: "When we have the impulse to say something, we inhale with the feeling of our response".[4] Imagine if someone told you had won the lottery. You would not take a neutral breath before exclaiming "I never have to work again!" No, the in-breath, and your physicality, would already carry the excitement of your expression. These are the processes Peter Brook was referring to when he said, "A word does not start as a word". Infuse your in-breath with whatever you are going to express.

The value of an external focus

To sing in this way requires a strong external focus on your character's reality. That requires the bravery to let go of any technical, internal thoughts that come from our work in Part I. Thinking technically about your posture or breathing is not only boring for an audience but doesn't help you as much as you may think. In fact, the reverse has been shown to be true: an external focus will make you sing better both artistically and technically. In 2019, a joint team from Munich and Las Vegas studied the effect of an expressive, external focus on musicians' performances.[5] Their participants gave three performances: one focusing on an internal aspect such as a pianist's fingers on keys or a trumpeter's embouchure; one focusing externally on their effect on the audience and musical expression; and a control where they did what they would usually do. The study concluded that the external focus produced superior performance in expression and technique compared to both the internal focus and control.

An external focus also allows you to create more exciting performances by reacting spontaneously to what is happening. The psychologist Mihalyi Csikzentmihalyi has spent much of his life studying creativity. His work has shown that artists who stick with their external focus can "learn from the emerging work; he or she is alert to the unexpected and is willing to go with a better solution if one presents itself."[6] They can react and create better works than those who stick rigidly to their internal plan. For us as performers, it is often more rewarding to work with someone who is alive to the possibilities being created in the moment of a scene or song. It is also important to keep spontaneity alive during a long run of a show.

One final piece of research examined the results of focusing on cause versus effect, that is, focusing on how you do something versus what you want to do.[7] In singing, that would be the cause of good singing – standing well, breathing well, etc. – versus the effect of good singing – changing the character's external or internal world. The researchers found that directing your body to *what* you want to happen rather than *how* it should happen was consistently better. So, once you have begun to embody the techniques in Part I, stop thinking about them and direct your attention instead to changing your character's world.

Maximising the impression

The next part of this chapter is going to help you train your imagination so that the Impression makes such an impact on you, it triggers all the physical responses of good singing and all the emotional, expressive ones. The director Declan Donnellan said, "Like the body, the imagination needs patience, training and endurance. As we have seen, we train the imagination only by letting ourselves see. Attention is our best coach."[8] What we see is the Impression and it has many characteristics. The first to consider is the pictures of your character's internal and external worlds.

Once you are in a full-scale production, the external world of your character and its Impressions will be created around you. Everything they can see, you will be able to see, via the scenery, costumes, props, and other characters. However, most of the time we will have to create this world for ourselves. When practising a song, rehearsing, auditioning, or giving a concert performance, the world of the character remains imaginary. To make the imaginary world as vibrant and affecting as possible, we create vivid mental pictures of the imaginary world. We will also have to do this for the character's internal world. In rehearsals, we may improvise scenes not in the show to enhance this internal world, for example, by playing the moments before a scene begins. But even here, it will be useful to have vivid pictures of your character's internal life.

Pictures are vital to Impressions. The Broadway casting director Michael Shurtleff wrote one of the finest books on acting and getting the job, called *Audition*. In it, he emphasises how important pictures are to the acting process: "In every new class I ask a student, 'Where were you on Sunday afternoon at three-thirty?' Almost invariably the actor will look away from me before he can answer; he must *see* where he was on Sunday at three-thirty, or he can't tell me. Acting is seeing. That's what images are: pictures of what did happen to us, pictures of what may happen to us in the future. We see our entire lives in images."[9]

Over the next two chapters, we're going to take a detailed look at the song "Precipice", with music by Adam Gerber and lyrics by Tori Allen-Martin. It's a new Musical Theatre piece about a character who gets caught up in a love affair while she and her lover are both in other relationships. Here are the lyrics in full:

> He... he has this way about him that makes me forget myself,
> We... we shouldn't be doing this, we should be somewhere else,
> I... I belong to someone else
> He belongs to someone else, too
> We should just forget all this.
> This love is an apocalypse.
> It's selfish and I'm foolish.
> He... he takes me to the brink, and then calms me down again,
> I used to be a better girl but I don't remember then,
> Everything before him disappeared, I don't know when,
> Here he comes again.
> And I'm on the edge of this precipice
> You could kill me with just one more kiss.
> And I should say no but if I let you go,
> It wouldn't stop me from falling,
> I can hear you calling,
> The only way is down for us now.
> I'm on the edge of this precipice,
> Wrong or right, I'm choosing this.
> Go on and kill me, just one more kiss.
> Falling off the edge of this precipice.
> Go on and kill me,
> I could get used to this.
> He... he's a cool wind on a hot day and I can't get enough,
> We're breaking other hearts, we went and played too rough.
> I belong to someone else, he belongs to someone else too
> We should just forget all this.
> This love is an apocalypse.
> It's selfish, and I'm foolish.
> And I'm on the edge of this precipice.
> You could kill me with just one more kiss.
> And I should say no but if I let you go,
> It wouldn't stop me from falling,
> I can hear you calling,
> The only way is down for us now.
> I'm on the edge of this precipice,
> Wrong or right, I'm choosing this.
> Go on and kill me, just one more kiss.
> Falling off the edge of this precipice.
> Go on and kill me,
> I could get used to this.
> And I'll break an innocent heart,
> But the feelings surge

I can't deny the urge to just blow everything apart,
For one more night with...
One more life with...
He... he has this way about him that makes me forget myself
I'm on the edge of the precipice,
Wrong or right, I'm choosing this.
Go on and kill me, just one more kiss.
Falling off the edge of this precipice.
Go on and kill me,
I could get used to this.
I'm on the edge of the precipice,
Wrong or right, I'm choosing this.
Go on and kill me, just one more kiss.

Now, let's do the work necessary to sing it brilliantly! This work can, and should, be applied to any song you sing. Firstly, you would need several pictures for the character's internal and external world. These include:

- your lover
- your partner
- your lover's partner
- memories of being with your lover physically and emotionally
- imagined scenes of telling your respective partners about the affair

But the pictures by themselves are not enough. The crucial element is to know how your character feels about those pictures. Then you can start to create relationships. Michael Shurtleff said "Creating relationship is the heart of acting. It is basic. It is essential."[10] Once you have a clear picture in your head of, say, your lover, that picture has to resonate with meaning for you otherwise it can never inspire you to sing.

As you sing a whole song, you journey through a series of emotionally resonant images. Declan Donnellan describes the process: "When we think, we see our thoughts... This thing that is seen is then discarded for something different that is seen and is then itself discarded, and so on. When I think, I reject one thought for another; I drop one thing I see for another thing I see. Thought is a process of discarding photographs. I see something and then what do I do? I ditch it for something else."[11] As long as you are seeing the images, and they resonate with you to a degree high enough to inspire singing, you will reach your audience. The musical side of your performance – the dynamics, vocal colours, etc. – will also develop naturally and effortlessly.

Let's continue with "Precipice". Here's the first part of the song with the pictures the text might inspire and their emotional resonances (Table 5.1).

Table 5.1 A table showing a breakdown of lyrics, along with the mental pictures they inspire and their emotional resonances

Text	Picture	Emotional resonance
He... he has this way about him that makes me forget myself	Your lover	Joy, love, wonder
We... we shouldn't be doing this, we should be somewhere else,	You and your lover together	Guilt but also desire
I... I belong to someone else	Your partner	Guilt, shame, but, crucially, an absence of the excitement and completeness you feel with your lover
He belongs to someone else, too	Your lover with his partner	Pain, anxiety
We should just forget all this. This love is an apocalypse. It's selfish and I'm foolish.	Breaking off the affair	Running away, overwhelmed, angry at yourself

Notice how we go through exactly the process of one image overtaking another. This leads us from joy to guilt to overwhelm, and this is only the first verse! But that's the level of story-telling Musical Theatre demands and it's your job as a singer to deliver that. Remember the advice of David Ostwald: "Imagine you are so deeply involved that your feelings cause you to utter sounds."[12]

It's worth noting that the ability to express emotions and tell stories is essential to making the transition from child-performer to professional adult-performer. In a major study on expert musicians, a team from Colorado and Berlin reported that the criteria by which children and adults are assessed changes in this way: "In the performance of music, children and adolescents are judged principally on their technical proficiency. Expert adult performers, however, are judged on their interpretation and ability to express emotions through music. The inability of many child prodigies in music to succeed as adult musicians is often attributed to difficulties making this transition".[13] So build your narrative ability because it's going to get you work. Stephen Sondheim said, "I generally prefer actors who can sing rather than a singer who can act...because I'm much more concerned with telling the story than I am with the enjoyment of the singing".[14]

What does your character want?

Impressions hit characters in an intense way because they affect what a character desires from life. When we see a character singing a song, "They appear to be living in the intersection where the input their senses receive crosses what they *want*".[15] Therefore, if you have an emotionally resonant image of what your character wants, it will elevate your performance.

What your character wants goes by many names: goal, objective, desire, intention, what they are fighting for. The important part is that you must find a clear relationship between the Impression that has caused you to sing and what you want. That relationship can be one of help or one of hindrance. Imagine you are playing Maria in *West Side Story* and all you've ever wanted is to be in love. The Impression of meeting Tony, the chemistry between you, the feelings that instantly bloom, put you on a rocket towards fulfilling that want. Much of the heartache in the rest of the show will come from the barriers to fulfilling that want. We will explore how the interaction of the Impression and what you want leads to Expression, later in this chapter.

A concept related to your character's desires is "the stakes". The stakes are whatever can be won from a situation and whatever can be lost. Sometimes the stakes are rooted in your character's primary intention, like when Sweeney Todd is about to take his revenge on the Judge by slitting his throat. Other times, the stakes are unexpectedly created in the moment, like Cinderella suddenly getting stuck on the steps of the palace. Either way, the stakes are always high. Always. If they weren't, your character would not be singing. Here's Broadway casting director Michael Shurtleff again: "you've watched people run for a subway: when they miss it and the door closes in their faces, they throw a fit screaming and cursing and stamping their feet. The fact that there's another subway coming along in seven minutes doesn't dampen their conduct. Right now, at this moment, catching that subway is the most important thing in the world. Will you do less than that for a scene in a play?... Make the stakes in each scene as high as you can. Look for the maximum importance. Add importance. If you don't, no one will be listening to you."[16]

Because the stakes are part of the Impression, they are something you can see. Director Declan Donnellan has an "unbreakable double rule" for seeing the stakes: "1. At every living moment there is something to be lost and something to be won. 2. The thing to be won is precisely the same size as the thing to be lost."[17] That means we should frame every stake as a double, with its positive and negative. For example, if we go back to Cinderella stuck on the steps of the palace, instead of seeing the stakes as "The Prince will discover me", we should frame them as "The Prince will discover me" *and* "the Prince will not discover me". The conflict of these opposites gives you more to play. Donnellan continues to explain: "It may tease and frustrate the actor to dig for this double, both the positive and the negative, but the positive in friction with the negative is precisely what sparks the actor."

Try this double framing with your own characters and songs and see what it brings to life for you.

Beats and events

Dividing your text into beats and events can be a useful way of ordering the Impressions on your character, making it easier for you to play them. "Beats" are the smaller changes that happen during the course of a scene or song. The concept originated with Stanislavski as the subdivision of a play's "units" and is now one of the most widely used in acting. Strangely, we may have the wrong word for this concept. Here's the director Katie Mitchell, in her book *The Director's Craft*:

> Stanislavsky himself never used this word. Instead he referred to these subdivisions as 'beads' (as in the beads a jeweller might thread together to make a necklace). Legend has it that Richard Boleslavsky, who taught Stanislavsky's system at the American laboratory theatre in the 1920s, had such a strong Polish accent that his students misheard the word 'bead' as 'beat'. It seems that we owe one of the most widely used terms of textual analysis in the western theatrical tradition to an error in pronunciation.[18]

The benefit of knowing about the "beads" is that it gives an image of continuity to these moments. By threading them together one by one, you create a whole piece. Whether you're thinking of beats or beads, the important point is to register the Impression of those moments. They change something in your character's world and she then has to deal with it.

Events are like beats but they reach further. Katie Mitchell gives this definition: "An event is the moment in the action when a change occurs and this change affects everyone present."[19] For example, when Valjean hears another man is going on trial for his crimes, that's a beat; when he walks into court and declares his true identity, everyone in that court is affected so that's an event.

Let's find the beats in the next part of "Precipice":

Beat 1: "I am deeply changed by my lover"

> He... he takes me to the brink, and then calms me down again,
> I used to be a better girl but I don't remember then,
> Everything before him disappeared, I don't know when,
> Here he comes again.

Beat 2: "I am helpless with you"

> And I'm on the edge of this precipice
> You could kill me with just one more kiss.
> And I should say no but if I let you go,
> It wouldn't stop me from falling,
> I can hear you calling,
> The only way is down for us now.

Beat 3: "I still want this"

> I'm on the edge of this precipice,
> Wrong or right, I'm choosing this.
> Go on and kill me, just one more kiss.
> Falling off the edge of this precipice.
> Go on and kill me,
> I could get used to this.

These three clear beats are three clear Impressions made on your character which cause her to sing. Take a song and explore the text in this way, marking out each of the beats.

Character history

Your character has a life history which influences the effect of Impressions. When Sally Bowles sings "Maybe This Time" in *Cabaret*, it means so much more to her because of a life history of failed romances. Opinions vary on how important it is for you to know the history of your character. Director Katie Mitchell devotes a significant amount of time to her actors' research. At the beginning of rehearsals, she asks them to make four lists on their character's history:

- facts about everything that exists and happens before the action of the play begins
- questions about everything that exists and happens before the action of the play begins
- facts about the immediate circumstances of the first scene
- questions about the immediate circumstances of the first scene[20]

This level of work will give you a highly detailed picture of your character's world. It's worth doing if you have the time and the performance warrants it. However, it is time consuming. It's unlikely you would do this for one audition where the panel only wants to hear a 32-bar cut.

The playwright and director David Mamet has the opposite perspective on Character History. He doesn't believe it even exists. In *True and False: Heresy and Common Sense for the Actor*, Mamet uses the following example. A director is researching a character in a play who has "been in Germany for some years." The director calls the playwright to ask just how many years. The playwright has no idea, and Mamet says we shouldn't expect him to: "The play is a fantasy, it is not a history. The playwright is not *withholding* information; he is *supplying* all the information he knows, which is to say, all the information that is germane. The character did not spend anytime *at all* in Germany. He never was *in* Germany. There *is* no character, there are just black marks on a white page – it is a line of dialogue... the character is just a sketch, a few lines on the pages; and to wonder of the character "How many years might he have spent in Germany?" is as pointless as to say of the subject of a portrait, "I wonder what underwear he has on?"[21]

Mamet's point here is that the only criterion that matters is how you finally play the scene. It's the action in the moment that counts, not the research beforehand. As he writes later, "It will not help you in the boxing ring to know the history of boxing".[22] You just have to see your opponent, trust your technique, and execute the actions that win the fight.

Conclusion

The Impression made on your character is what stimulates them to sing. We, as performers, have to exercise our imaginations to the level of intensity necessary to provoke that same reaction. More than that, we have to react with the length, pitch, and intensity of sound dictated by the composer. Director Declan Donnellan wrote about an actress struggling to take enough breath for a line of dialogue: "...her imagination needs to be acute enough to see the target that will make her react with that many words."[23] It's even more true for singers. The Impression has to trigger a big enough reaction in you to react not just with that many words, but that many words, at that pitch, sustained for that length of time. That's how you move beyond speaking to singing.

Here's a summary of what we have learnt so far in this chapter.

- The Impression is always a vivid image.
- Your character has a highly emotional relationship with that image.
- Images pile up over each other during the course of a song.
- The emotional resonance of the image is determined by what your character wants, both long term and immediately.
- The Impression conveys that something is at stake to win and to lose.
- The stakes can be expressed in both positive and negative form, creating a dramatic friction for you to play.
- Beats and events in the text mark a change in the Impression or your character's reaction to the Impression.
- Character histories can enhance the importance of Impressions or you can play the immediacy of the scene.

★★★

Expression

Now we can move on to the other half of this partnership: Expression. In singing, the Expression is always urgent and vital. This manifests in your performance as an attempt to change or celebrate the Impression. There are four scenarios you could play:

- the outside world isn't doing what I want so I need to change it
- my internal world isn't structured as I want so I need to change it
- the outside world is exactly what I want so I'm going to celebrate it
- my internal world is exactly what I want so I'm going to celebrate it

Often, the first two come as a pair, as do the second two, because of the effect of outside events on your character's internal world. Let's take some examples.

The outside world isn't doing what I want so I need to change it

In *Little Women*, Jo, an aspiring writer, often faces difficulties in the outside world that she wants to change. At the beginning of the show, she receives another rejection letter from a publisher. After getting an unfavourable opinion from a professor, she sings "Better". Later, when she rejects a marriage proposal, she again confronts an outside world that is failing to meet her desires and sings "Astonishing".

80 *Expressive Singing*

My internal world isn't structured as I want so I need to change it

In *Newsies The Musical*, the young reporter Katherine sees an opportunity to cover the story of the newsboys' strike and boost her career. When she sings "Watch What Happens", she is clearly struggling with her own internal doubts. She then attempts to change her internal world so that she has the courage to cover the story.

The outside world is exactly what I want so I'm going to celebrate it

In *Amelie*, the eponymous heroine celebrates moving to Paris, finding an apartment, and living the life she has dreamed of. As the outside world lines up just as she wants, she sings "Times are Hard for Dreamers" to celebrate.

My internal world is exactly what I want so I'm going to celebrate it

In *My Fair Lady*, Eliza dances with Professor Higgins during "The Rain in Spain". That experience leads to her internal world clicking into place and so she sings "I Could Have Danced All Night" as she celebrates the new emotions she's feeling.

Whichever scenario or combination of scenarios you are playing, you must play it with total commitment. Thomas Hemsley said good singing belongs to those who, "with their entire being, wish to share their thoughts and feelings."[24]

Let's dig into this a bit more by looking at the first scenario: changing the outside world. Broadway casting director Michael Shurtleff said actors should imbue every scene with two perspectives: "1. I am right and you are wrong. 2. You should change from being the way you are to be what I think you should be."[25] This double-perspective should drive your engagement with the scene or song. It's especially useful when the thing about the outside world you are trying to change is a person (which, in songs, it often is). Imagine singing "Don't Rain on My Parade". You are furiously trying to change Mr Arnstein because he is wrong and you are right. Or "You Don't Know This Man" from *Parade*. The title shows that you think the reporter Britt Craig is wrong about your husband and that you are right. Or "Right Hand Man" from *Something Rotten!* Bea is desperate to convince her husband that she can fill the traditionally male role of one of his friends. Shurtleff advises viewing this kind of engagement as a competition: "...without competition between the characters, drama is dull indeed, since it feeds on conflict, and dies with agreement...the good actor is one who competes, willingly, who *enjoys* competing... an actor must compete, or die."[26] This reinforces why the Impression must be so earth-shattering: because it has to inspire the "compete or die" mentality in your performance.

The remaining scenarios need the same high level of emotional engagement. Even if the end goal is to express joy at things going right, rather than changing a character to act as you want, it's still an intense, urgent, and vital form of expression. Here's an exercise to help.

Stand up and look out of a window. Imagine someone you love is standing outside, preferably by a road but any location will do. Now imagine they are about to be run down by a bus. Call out to them on the word "hey" to save their life. The person you love and the oncoming bus are the Impression; your "hey" is the Expression. If your "hey" was timid, shy, quiet, then your loved one got squished. Sorry. If your "hey" was kind of loud but not really, they still got squished. It has to be urgent. When you do this right, the "hey" will feel like a long, resonant call. The Impression will trigger all the habits of good singing and you will make an engaged, supported sound. It should not hurt your throat at all. If it does, something is wrong so reset and build up again. You can rate your "hey" on an intensity level from 1 to 10. It's difficult to convey these levels in a book, but they should feel something like the following table (Table 5.2).

Remember, singing starts when speech is no longer enough. That means you have to reach the highest intensity of speaking – levels 9–10 – before you break through to the lowest intensity of singing.

Now take that intensity rating and apply it to a line of text from a song. Songs with big final lines often work well, such as "Woman" from *The Pirate Queen*, "Defying Gravity" from *Wicked*, "Watch What Happens" from *Newsies*, or "Astonishing" from *Little Women*. Whichever song

Table 5.2 Increasing levels of emotional intensity. Try to build up to a 10, feeling emotionally engaged and vocally healthy

Level 1	"hey" – like you're a bit down and you're greeting a stranger
Level 5	"Hey" – assertive but lacking urgency and fullness
Level 7	"Heeey" – the urgency is building and you're producing a longer fuller sound
Level 8	"Heeeey!" – starting to feel like you really mean it
Level 9	"HEEEEEEY!" Urgent, full, supported, engaged
Level 10	"HEEEEEEEEEEEEEY!!" a sound from your very core, made with your entire being

you choose, speak the lines dramatically. Now give yourself an intensity rating on a scale of 1–10. Remember how close you got to the "HEEEEEEEEEEY!!" Once you're at a 9, speak the line again but stay on one pitch. Lengthen the words so that they match the rhythm of the music. Remember you have to find the emotional engagement necessary to sustain a sound for the length of time a composer wants it. The last word in the text of "Woman" is 16 beats long plus a pause. That's about 7 seconds on one word. When you speak this on pitch, try to find the emotional energy necessary to sustain that word meaningfully for 7 seconds. Finally, put the tune back in, but don't discard all the work you've just done. Don't go back to singing it as you would have before. Maintain the emotional engagement of these words and move from pitch to pitch almost as if it were a coincidence that you are singing the melody the composer has written. The important thing is to maintain your vital, urgent communication.

What you are doing here is stretching your emotional muscles. Just like physical muscles, stretching them means there is a greater capacity available to you. When you go into an audition, you can hit your 9/10 intensity immediately, rather than delivering a lukewarm 7. By the way, I say 9/10, so you leave room to crank it up to a 10 later in the song. That's about all the dynamic journey we need in a song, but we'll discuss that in the next chapter, "Words and Music".

Once you are used to hitting that 9/10 intensity, you have two choices: you can deliver that 9/10 exactly as it is; or you can compress it. In her book on theatre, Anne Bogart quotes the Japanese actor and playwright Zeami, who lived over 600 years ago. He said: "When you feel ten in your heart, express seven."[27] This is compression. Bogart explains: "Expression is the result of containing, shaping and embodying the excitement that boils up inside of you." I like this idea. At times, expressing a 9/10 can be a bit much. Also, compressing those emotions gives them a concentrated quality. Whether you choose the all-out 9 or the compressed 7 may depend on your song. There's no compression happening at the end of "Rain on My Parade" but it would work very well in "You Don't Know This Man". The choice is up to you.

Songs are your character's solution to getting what they want

In the Impression section, we did a lot of work on establishing what your character wants. Your singing should be the response to that. Singing is a powerful action taken by the character to fulfil their desires.

Take *The Sound of Music*, for example. Maria wants to find her place in the world. The nuns want that for her, too, and they suspect it is not going to be in the Abbey. Liesel wants to explore falling in love and becoming a young woman. The children want attention, play, learning, and a relationship with their father. During the show, they all do many things to achieve their goals and singing is one of, if not the, most important. When Liesel sings "Sixteen Going on Seventeen", every word and sound is an attempt to make Rolf fall in love with her. When Maria sings "My Favourite Things", every word and sound tries to comfort the children and make them feel calm during the storm.[ii] When you think of a song as an action to achieve a goal, it takes on a greater motivation which drives your performance. Watching this drive on stage or during an audition is part of the excitement of watching singing.

Thinking of songs as actions also helps prioritise your voice when you perform. I often see young singers doing plenty of story-telling with their facial expressions and their gestures, but the best singers are doing it with voice. Every word they utter and every sound they make carries meaning and intention. That's the job of a singer.

Some notes on acting

Now that we've taken care of the big acting processes, here are some notes on acting that can help guide your choices.

If there's something likeable available in a character, play it

We're attracted to characters who show virtues: courage, strength, wit, humour, joy, honesty, etc. If you can find that in your character, play it. For example, when Cathy sings "Still Hurting", you could make the choice to play her as defeated, weak, miserable, and bitter, but who would sympathise with that character and want to watch the rest of the show? Better to make her strong even in her heartbreak, loving in her anger, and honest in her confusion. I watched a student give a performance of "All Falls Down" from *Chaplin: The Musical* that was vocally fine but full of sass and bitterness to the exclusion of anything likeable. Once we explored the depth of the character and found her wit and strength, the performance lifted significantly.

---

ii In the film version. In the original stage version, she sings "The Lonely Goatherd".

Play opposites

"Excess of sorrow laughs. Excess of joy weeps."[28] So wrote the great English poet, William Blake. We have all experienced this. People cry at weddings because they're so happy. And when one bad thing happens after another, sometimes you just have to laugh. These opposites are worth remembering and playing. If you were singing "I Don't Know How to Love Him" from *Jesus Christ Superstar*, maybe Mary Magdalen is so upset during the middle section that she laughs about it. And if you were singing, "Till There Was You" from *The Music Man*, what it would be like to enter the middle section so overwhelmed by happiness that there are tears in your eyes?

Play time and place

Time is a vital part of a character's experience. The romance between Usnavi and Vanessa in *In The Heights* is intensified by the time pressure of Usnavi's one-way flight out of the country. The whole show is set in a time of year with a scorching summer that affects all the characters. Director Katie Mitchell says, "The playing of time is often neglected. You see scenes in some productions in which the writer intends that the characters are talking whilst operating under a time pressure where one actor is playing it and the other is not, or no one is playing it at all. This gives conflicting information to the audience... Deciding on the time at which each scene is set helps you to avoid this sort of problem."[29]

When thinking about time, consider absolute time and relative time. Absolute time includes the time of day, time of year, season, weekday, and weekend. Relative time is the amount of time a character has left before an event.

Consider place, as well. Where is your song taking place? Can you see the palace in *The King and I*, the farm in *Oklahoma*, or the decrepit mansion in *Sunset Boulevard*? Seeing it clearly is only the first step; then you must find how you feel about the place. Here's Michael Shurtleff: "Take your own apartment: when you first look at it, you are uncertain: Should you rent this place, or should you not? Will you like it, or won't you? Can you afford it? Then you settle in, fix it up, make it suitable for you, and you like it a lot. Install a lover, and when he leaves, you'll hate the place you liked before. All the same place, but how you feel about it changes depending on the emotional events that take place there."[30] It's the feelings that attach to a place that give you an "emotional value" to play.

Gesture

Here's a rule I make in my classes: no half gestures. You often see a singer performing and, every now and then, her hand makes a small gesture, usually at the waistline. She spreads open her palms or points a finger or clenches a fist. Avoid these half gestures. They read as indecision and lack of commitment. As David Ostwald said: "If a gesture is worth doing, it generally should be done with your hands above the waist."[31] So if you are going to gesture, make it clear and commit to it. Ostwald also advises you to go with your gut: "like most performers, you probably have good natural instincts about when to gesture, particularly as you begin to get into a role. Therefore, when you feel the slightest impulse to gesture in a rehearsal...act on it. Any gesture will do to begin with. As you continue to rehearse, bearing in mind that audiences read every gesture as a significant piece in the puzzle they are assembling, you can refine them and decide how long to sustain them or how subtly to shape them; you may also decide to eliminate some as superfluous or repetitive. Ultimately you want to be sure that each one is evocative." As a general rule, a few bold gestures read better than lots of little ones. As a director once said to me, "Do less, and do it bigger."

Half gestures are a type of "physical noise". Physical noise is extraneous movement that clouds the clear and direct communication coming from your body. Another type of physical noise is shuffling your feet. Some performers take little steps back and forth, or side to side, as they perform, especially in a scene with other people. It adds nothing; in fact it distracts. Aim for physically noiseless performances. That way, your communication will be direct and full of impact.

Mystery, magnetism, and humour

The great performances have everything we have discussed so far but they also have these three qualities: magnetism, mystery, and humour.

Singer Thomas Hemsley said magnetism is "perhaps the greatest gift a singer can have."[32] It is that quality in a performance which draws the audience in, which makes an audience member believe they alone are being sung to by the performer. Can it be learnt? Some people will say that magnetism, like charisma, is something you are born with and can never be learned. I disagree. You can create the conditions in which magnetism can arise. Helpfully, Hemsley outlined some dos and don'ts:

- Don't be self-conscious or self-absorbed. Thinking about your sound, or the reaction of the audience, or how much you want the audition, only takes you away from communicating the song. This then takes you away from an audience.

- Don't go into a performance under-prepared. Know your music, know your text, know your Impressions and everything that goes with them.
- Don't fall out of the dramatic moment. It's so easy to think "that big note's coming up", or "this is going really well" or "really badly", but, again, these thoughts only take you away from communicating the song. Stick to your actions and see if they are changing the world as your character wishes.
- Don't aim to touch an audience. That might be the end goal but we can't rush to it just like we can't rush up to someone and declare: "I really want to be friends with you!"; you have to do the things that make you friends instead. We can only offer everything we've outlined in this book and then it's up to the audience to choose to accept it. Allow your audience to come to you, don't go to them.
- Do perform with a noiseless, toned, vibrant posture.
- Do thoroughly prepare.
- Do let your imagination lead, expressing the narrative of your Impressions.
- Do share. "The mental attitude of wishing to share your experience of the poetry, the drama, and the music, with the audience, and to establish a relationship with the audience by drawing them towards you. Closely associated with this is perhaps the most important of all: sheer joy in the act of singing and sharing."[33]

The concepts of mystery and humour are both to be found in Michael Shurtleff's *Audition*. "Mystery" is a sense of wonder and awe at the unknowable internal world of another person and at our character's own internal world. We do so much preparation on songs, characters, circumstances, and the rest, that we often forget to leave room for the mystery of what we do not know. Shurtleff says: "no matter how much we know about the other person, there is always something going on in that other heart and that other head that we don't know but can only ponder. And no matter how we explain ourselves to someone else, no matter how open we are, there is always still something inexplicable, something hidden and unknown in us, too."[34] Trust this mystery; let it play in your performances. If you perform thinking you know everything about the situation, you'll get bored and the vitality of your performance will be dimmed.

Finally, when asked what is the outstanding trait he looks for in performers, the man who was the Broadway casting director for *Chicago*,

Pippin, Gypsy, The Sound of Music, and *Jesus Christ Superstar*, answered: "humour". "I doubt there has ever been an outstanding actor who was humourless. Humour is the most private, most distinctive, most personal of all human traits. It is what makes each of us distinct."[35] Humour doesn't mean the ability to make people laugh. It's a heightened sense of perception, and an attitude of sharing, communication and enjoyment. These are qualities we can all develop. As Shurtleff concludes, "Nobody would want to live in a humourless world. Why would anyone want a humourless actor?"

Summing-up

This has been a big chapter. We've explored the concepts of Impression and Expression: two worlds that exist on an in-breath and an out-breath. They are the worlds an audience comes to be part of and that we performers have the privilege of creating. Enjoy the processes we have explored, play with them, and have fun.

At the end of the process comes the product and that's what we turn to in our final chapter, "Words and Music".

Notes

1 Brook, P. (1968) *The Empty Space*, Penguin, p. 15.
2 Donnellan, D. (2005) *The Actor and the Target*, New Edition, Nick Hern Books, p. 200.
3 Hemsley, T. (1998) p. 41, including Manén, L. (1987) *Bel Canto*, OUP.
4 Ostwald, D.F. (2005) *Acting for Singers: Creating Believable Singing Characters*, OUP, p. 18.
5 Mornell, A. and Wulf, G. (2019) "Adopting an External Focus of Attention Enhances Musical Performance", *Journal of Research in Music Education*, 66:4, 375–391.
6 Csikszentmihalyi, M. (1997) *Creativity: The Psychology of Discovery and Invention*, Harper, p. 367.
7 Lewthwaite, R. and Wulf, G. (2017) "Optimizing Motivation and Attention for Motor Performance and Learning", *Current Opinion in Psychology*, 16, 38–42.
8 Donnellan, D. (2005), p. 157.
9 Shurtleff, M. (1978) *Audition: Everything an Actor Needs to Know to Get the Part*, Bloomsbury, p. 116.
10 Ibid., p. 23.
11 Donnellan, D. (2005), p. 189.
12 Ostwald, D.F. (2005), p. 12.
13 Ericsson, K.A., Krampe, R.T. and Tesch-Romer, C. (1993) "The Role of Deliberate Practice in the Acquisition of Expert Performance", *Psychological Review*, 100:3, 369.

14 Sondheim, S. in an interview with the US Library of Congress, 06/02/2017. Retrieved at https://www.loc.gov/static/programs/national-recording-preservation-board/documents/SondheimInterview.pdf
15 Ostwald, D.F. (2005), p. 20.
16 Shurtleff, M. (1978), p. 67–68.
17 Donnellan, D. (2005), p. 51.
18 Mitchell, K. (2009) *The Director's Craft: A Handbook for the Theatre*, Routledge, p. 226.
19 Ibid., p. 55.
20 Ibid., p. 143.
21 Mamet, D. (1997) *True and False: Heresey and Common Sense for the Actor*, Random House, pp. 60–61.
22 Ibid., p. 62.
23 Donnellan, D. (2005), p. 157.
24 Hemsley, T. (1998), p. 31.
25 Shurtleff, M. (1978), p. 65.
26 Ibid., pp. 65–66.
27 Bogart, A. (2001), p. 144.
28 Blake, W. *The Marriage of Heaven and Hell*, "Proverbs of Hell" Plate 8.
29 Mitchell, K. (2009), p. 40.
30 Shurtleff, M. (1978), p. 82.
31 Ostwald, D.F. (2005), p. 185.
32 Hemsley, T. (1998), p. 187.
33 Ibid., pp. 188–189.
34 Shurtleff, M. (1978), p. 94.
35 Ibid., p. 154.

6 Words and Music

In 1774, Giambattista Mancini wrote: "An actor or singer cannot express passions and feelings nor transmit them to the public if he does not comprehend the value and meaning of each word".[1] This remains true, today, so the first thing we are going to do in this chapter is to ensure that every single word you sing is full of meaning.

First of all, you need to know the objective (literal) meaning of every word you're singing. Then you need to know the subjective meaning – how your character feels about the word – because that gives the word its emotional value. For example, if you are singing "I'd Give My Life For You" from *Miss Saigon*, the word "war" is going to have a specific feeling for Kim, who has seen war ravage her country, much more than for someone who has never experienced it. Pictures are once again a must. When Kim sings the word "him", you must see pictures of Chris and all the love and desire connected with him.

Here's an exercise to maximise your engagement with the words. Go through your text one word at a time and make sure you have a feeling, and preferably a picture too, attached to each word. All the little words are just as important so include every "as", "in", "of", "my", "for", and "to" in this exercise. Firstly, clarify your objective and subjective meanings. In the example below, I've continued using "Precipice", moving from the emotional pictures we created in the previous chapter to detailed, specific meanings on every word. The subjective meanings here are just one interpretation, you can make your own (Table 6.1).

Once you are clear on the meanings and the associated pictures, say the word out loud and convey that meaning only through the sounds of the word, remembering what we said in the previous chapter about using words as actions to get what you want. When you say the word "We", all you have is the two vowel sounds "ooh" and "ee" that make up the diphthong of the word "we' to convey "Two people who should have known better and been more responsible". Similarly, when you say

DOI: 10.4324/9781003286875-9

Table 6.1 The text of a song, word by word, with objective and subjective meanings

Text	Objective Meaning	Subjective Meaning
We're	Me and my lover	The two of us together and what we do when we're together
Breaking	Hurting	Knowingly, guiltily hurting
Other	Our respective partners	Our partners who are innocent, who we promised to be faithful to
Hearts	Emotional state of our partners	The core of their being, the most important and most vulnerable part of them
We	Me and my lover	Two people who should have known better and been more responsible
Went	Carried on	Acted even though we knew it was wrong
And	And	Even more than that
Played	Got physically and emotionally close	Fell in love
Too	Too much	Crossed a line
Rough	Dangerously	Now people will get hurt

"rough", you have the "r" and "f" consonants, plus the vowel in between to convey "now people will get hurt". (I'm not suggesting you separate these sounds as you say them, I just want to be clear that you will bring all the sounds to life by investing them with meaning.) Go through the whole line like this, one word at a time. You should build up a clear emotional response to each word. Once you have, run each word after the other. This should not sound like a naturalistic line reading. Rather, it will be a line where every word is given its own individual emphasis. (It might sound a bit like old computer speech programmes.) Finally, go back to singing the line but, crucially, retain your emotional connection to every word. You should find you are now considerably more engaged emotionally and physically with the song.

Repeat this process enough so that your base-level of engagement with words is much higher, that is, until you naturally start giving this level of meaning to each word. Director Anne Bogart said

"The act of speaking becomes dramatic because of the change that occurs inside the person who is present, in the moment, engaged in speech."[2] Those changes occur because of the meaning and attachments of each word.

This level of engagement with the words demands all your attention. All your focus is on meaning and whether that meaning is getting through to your character's external or internal world. Then you have no mental space leftover to think about how you sound, or how the audition's going, or any of that. That's how it should be because you can be thinking about singing or you can be singing; but you cannot be doing both. Director Peter Brook once said of a performance, "…it was perfect because he had no attention spare for self-consciousness".[3] That's what we are aiming for.

This way of working can also smarten up your diction. Singing clear words should come from a desire to communicate every thought and feeling to your audience. By committing to every sound that transmits your meaning, you hit every vowel and consonant in a clear, resonant way.

It's worth remembering that the way you deal with words in a line in singing is different to spoken acting. In spoken acting, you can decide which words are important and deserve to be emphasised – "To be, or *not* to be"; "To *be*, or not to *be*", etc. – but in singing that decision has already been made by the composer. We all sing "Happy *birthday to you*" – and not "*Happy* birthday *to* you" – because that's how the rhythm has been set. When you sing, you don't add inflections to the line as you would in a play because the inflections are already there. What you have to do as a singer is realise the entire line. Then, by giving Mancini's "value and meaning to each word", we will hear the inflection written into the music. If you go for words that already have a musical stress and ignore the ones that don't, your phrasing will become lumpy.

Once we have every word clear in every line, we can start chunking them together to make verses. We use the word "verse" when talking about songs but if we were discussing poetry, we might use the word "stanza". Stanza is an Italian word which means "room" so moving through the stanzas of a poem is like moving through the rooms of a house.[4] Each room has its particular feeling and atmosphere. By encountering each one, you get to know the whole house. It's exactly the same for a song. Let's continue our study of "Precipice" to see how we can put this into practice. I have broken down some of the lyrics into their stanzas and moods (Table 6.2).

92 *Expressive Singing*

Table 6.2 Stanzas and Moods. This table takes blocks of text – stanzas – and identifies their moods

Stanza	Mood
He… he has this way about him that makes me forget myself, We… we shouldn't be doing this, we should be somewhere else, I… I belong to someone else He belongs to someone else, too	Struggling: she doesn't know how to deal with wanting her lover while knowing she should be faithful to her partner
We should just forget all this. This love is an apocalypse. It's selfish and I'm foolish.	Defeated: she gives up on their relationship because the situation is too difficult
He… he takes me to the brink, and then calms me down again,	Passionate
I used to be a better girl but I don't remember then, Everything before him disappeared, I don't know when,	Confused, unsure
Here he comes again.	In love

This opening can be broken down into five stanzas (rooms), each with its own mood. If you as a singer can take us through each of those rooms, making distinct the different moods, then you will deliver a very clear piece of story-telling. We will see the mental and emotional journey of the character.

This process also strengthens the in-breath we discussed in the previous chapter. Remember the quote from David Ostwald, "When we have the impulse to say something, we inhale with the feeling of our response"? Well, the feeling of the stanza is the feeling of your response. So you breathe in on that and ride every breath of that stanza in the same way. Then you change for the first breath of the next stanza and ride that new feeling. You continue this through the song, working Impression-Expression at the level of the stanza.

Go on stage and say the lines

Now that we have the highly detailed work of every word in every line, which is nested inside the larger feeling attached to a whole stanza, all that is left for you to do is to go on stage and deliver the words and notes. This can make us uncomfortable because it can feel like we are not doing enough to make the performance interesting. We might question our use of dynamics, phrasing, and registers. But don't question these things. Trust the material. I only met Stephen Sondheim once and it was very brief. He had given an interview in front of a live audience at the Cheltenham Literature Festival in 2010. Afterwards, he signed copies of the first volume of his lyrics *Finishing the Hat*. As I reached the front of the queue and handed over my copy to be autographed, I asked if he had any advice for singing his songs. His reply was simple: "Trust the songs." Playwright and director, David Mamet, gives the same advice to actors:

> "...*the words are set and unchanging. Any worth in them was put there by the author. His or her job is done, and the best service you can do them is to accept the words as is, and speak them simply and clearly in an attempt to get what you want from the other actor. If you learn the words by rote, as if they were a phone book, and let them come out of your mouth without your interpretation, the audience will be well served.*"[5]

As long as your whole body is engaged, and you express words with meaning on the pitches and rhythms written by the composer, then you have done your job. See what the character sees and say what the character says.

Sing the sentence, not the musical phrase

In a song, a single sentence can happen over many musical phrases. Think of the work we've done on "Precipice" and the line "And I should say no but if I let you go, it wouldn't stop me from falling...". Musically, the word "it" starts a new phrase by repeating the long note we heard at the beginning of the chorus a few lines earlier. Lyrically, however, "it" continues the sentence, and the thought, from "but if I let you go" on to "it wouldn't stop me from falling". It's very tempting to sing the musical phrases rather than the sentence, but the sentence carries the sense, and that's what's important. So when you start any sentence in a song, make sure you know where it ends and how far it travels to get there. It is imperative that you speak your text sentence by sentence so that you feel your character's thoughts unfolding.

A related issue here is rests. Rests can separate two musical phrases even when the character is in the middle of a sentence. In this instance, you have to keep thinking across the rest between "let you go" and "it wouldn't stop" so that you maintain the sense of the line. There is a crotchet rest between them but your character is still thinking and feeling her way through the sentence and so you must stay in that thought-feeling process. This often happens in singing because thoughts are unfurling very slowly. Speaking the lyrics to most songs takes a fraction of the time it takes to sing them. So lengthen your thought process so that it stretches out for as long as the lyric is suspended over the music.

Prioritise language over music. If we compare the units of each we have words, sentences, and text, and notes, phrases, and music. Sing words rather than notes; sing sentences rather than phrases; and sing text rather than music.

Beginning a song

The beginning of a song is the moment to connect with your audience and embark on the narrative journey you are about to take with them. But do not take their attention for granted. "We cannot assume that the audience will assemble devoutly and attentively. It is up to us to capture its attention and compel its belief", wrote director Peter Brook.[6] Here are a few tips to help you do that.

Firstly, present your character fully from the moments before the music starts. All the imaginative work you have done on the Impression, words, character history, intentions, and all the rest, has to switch on immediately so that the audience can enter the scene. Michael Shurtleff wrote: "There is little time for builds and explorations; the actor has to be there with the feeling from the top, or the scene is over with and gone by."[7]

Secondly, don't start too quietly. Many singers start songs too quietly in the mistaken belief that starting soft and finishing loud creates a narrative journey. It doesn't. A narrative journey is not a journey of dynamics; it's a journey of thoughts and feelings. When you start a song, more often than not, you can start with a full, confident tone, around mezzo-forte (moderately loud) in dynamic. By doing this, you present yourself to an audience as someone who knows what they are doing and has something interesting to say.

Thirdly, perform to someone specific. Imagine someone out in the audience or audition room with whom you can create a loving, communicative relationship. This will add warmth to your performance.

Lastly, don't get tricked by the music. There are plenty of songs that start slowly or sadly or mournfully. That kind of music does not supply you with the physical energy necessary to sing so don't get caught up in it. You have to summon up that toned, 9/10 physical-emotional engagement, despite the music. Have you ever noticed that up-tempo songs can be easier to sing? That's partly because the music in those does supply you with the right energy. So whatever the intro, whether it's the aching chords of "I Dreamed a Dream" or the bubbly waltz of "I Don't Know What I'd Do Without You", be in the high intensity state necessary for singing.

Sing it the way the composer wrote it

It's true that different forms of music have different levels of adherence to the written score. Classical music is the strictest, with singers permitted almost no deviation from the composer's wishes. Musical Theatre is more flexible. There is room for the singer's interpretation in a rhythm or melody. The amount of room can depend on the show. A singer would usually be allowed more freedom in a pop/rock musical than in a legit musical.

However, composers often like songs to be performed the way they wrote them. I coached a student on a song which she then performed for the composer. He praised her for realising more of his intentions in the song than anyone else he had heard perform it. In an interview with the BBC, composer John Kander was asked about his favourite performances of his work. He talked about Dame Judi Dench as Sally Bowles in *Cabaret* and Liza Minelli's recording of "New York, New York" and in both cases he praised them for singing it "the way we wrote it".[8]

To combine these two approaches, learn the song exactly as it is on the page. You will often find there is plenty of drama in strictly following the composer's setting. Once you have internalised that, you can begin to play with your interpretation. Just remember that if you change something, you must have a highly credible dramatic reason for so doing.

Rhythm

"In the beginning was rhythm." That saying is credited to the 19th century conductor and piano virtuoso Hans von Bülow.[9] Rhythm is often seen as the most important element of music, even more so than melody and harmony. Rhythm is based on a beat or pulse. Without a pulse, the music is dead. Strengthening the rhythms in your songs will elevate your performances. Here are some tips.

Work with a metronome. I cannot overstate the importance of this. Metronomes give you a clear, stable, indefatigable beat. You should be able to speak all your lyrics to the beat of a metronome with precision timing. Metronomes are easily, and feely, downloadable to a tablet or smartphone. Get one and start working with it.

When you are speaking your text to a metronome, you have two choices about the relationship of the words to the beat. You can either put the vowel on the beat or the consonant. As a general rule, put the vowel on the beat and get the consonant early.

As an example, let's look at the first line of the old, English tongue twister, "Peter Piper":

Peter Piper picked a peck of pickled peppers.

Now, let's mark the beat with an asterisk (Figure 6.1).

Beat: *   *   *   *   *   *

Line: P<u>e</u>ter P<u>i</u>per p<u>i</u>cked a p<u>e</u>ck of p<u>i</u>ckled p<u>e</u>ppers.

Figure 6.1 Putting the vowel on the beat.

Delivered like this, the performer creates an energetic and exciting rhythm with a sense of leading the beat. Try it and clap your hands on the beat. Make sure your vowels, not your consonants, are landing on the clapped beats.

Now look at the version where the consonant is on the beat (Figure 6.2).

Delivered like this, the performer is late. She will fall behind the beat and the rhythm will be sloppy and undramatic.

Take the time to practise your rhythms to a metronome and get the vowel on the beat. Useful songs to try this with include "Getting Married Today" (the quick, patter section) from *Company*, "Words, Words, Words" from *The Witches of Eastwick*, and "If You Hadn't, But You Did" from *Two on the Aisle*.

Styles

Musical Theatre has now been around long enough to have developed distinct styles of show and you should have a grasp of what each style requires from its singers. The most common styles are legit, contemporary legit, contemporary, and rock/pop. Sometimes more than one style of singing comes up in the same show, like in *Oklahoma* where

Beat: *   *   *   *   *   *

Line: <u>P</u>eter <u>P</u>iper <u>p</u>icked a <u>p</u>eck of <u>p</u>ickled <u>p</u>eppers.

Figure 6.2 Putting the consonant on the beat.

Laurie is a heady soprano and Ado Annie a character belt. For singers, this presents a difficult balancing act between knowing your casting type and being prepared to sing for any role. Versatility is a strength and will make you more employable. On the other hand, singers who have a clear and distinct type can have a long and rewarding career in a narrow range of roles.

In 2014, a team from Shenandoah University in Virginia published some research into what styles of show were auditioning in the United States, including on Broadway, US tours, and cruise ships, over a six-month period.[10] Here's what they found:

- 45% traditional/legit: e.g., *Phantom of the Opera, South Pacific, Hello, Dolly,* and *Chicago*
- 30% contemporary: e.g., *The Book of Mormon, The Lion King, Matilda,* and *Wicked*
- 25% pop/rock: e.g., *Jersey Boys, Mamma Mia,* and *We Will Rock You*

That's a pretty even spread so as a performer you need to be able to sing each style, otherwise you are writing off a lot of work. Remember, though, that the majority of what you do to sing well stays the same regardless of style. Whether you are singing *Cinderella* or *Motown the Musical*, you still need whole-body engagement, placement, Impression-Expression, and all the rest of the things we've explored in this book. These are the structures of good singing. You will also have to perform eight shows a week, whichever show you are in, so you have to sing healthily.

When students leave an MT degree programme, they usually have a rep folder with a go-to song for each style. This is very important and having a broad rep folder shows your versatility. However, this is again a balancing act. You should also know which rep suits you. Do you shine in the contemporary belt repertoire, or can you riff clearly and excitingly, or have you got exquisite heady top notes? Choosing the wrong rep holds you back but choosing the right rep enhances your performance.

Italian terms

Lots of songs still have Italian musical terms printed on them, like "allegro", "poco crescendo", etc. It's part of your job to know what these mean. It also takes about 10 seconds to search the Internet for the answers so there's no excuse for not doing this work.

Summing-up

Words and Music are our end-products. They need the attention of the craftswoman, making sure of tuning, timing, and diction; and they need the attention of the artist, filling them with meaning and expression. Ultimately, these two are not separate. They come from one, unified person: you, the singer.

Notes

1. Mancini, G. (1774) *Practical Reflections on the Figurative Art of Singing*, translated by Pietro Buzzi, p. 167.
2. Bogart, A. (2001), p. 65.
3. Brook, P. (1968), p. 28.
4. I first encountered this idea in the writings of US Poet Laureate Billy Collins but have been unable to track down the reference.
5. Mamet, D. (1997), pp. 62–63.
6. Brook, P. (1968), p. 108.
7. Shurtleff, M. (1978), pp. 146–147.
8. "Front Row", BBC Radio 4, broadcast 24/12/2014, available on BBCSounds.
9. Walker, A. (1988) *Franz Liszt: The Weimar Years, 1848–1861*, Cornell University Press, p. 175.
10. Green, K., Freeman, W., Edwards, M. and Meyer, D. (2014) "Trends in Musical Theatre Voice: An Analysis of Audition Requirements for Singers", *Journal of Voice*, 28:3, 324–327.

Final Thoughts

I am always happy to see a student grow and develop. I hope the ideas and exercises in this book have helped your development and will inform your ongoing learning, practising, and performing.

We have built your singing from the ground up, literally, starting with the connection between your feet and the floor. We established your posture, breathing, and placement. We found the trigger for these in the Impression, with its external and internal images, stakes, character, beats, and events. This led us to Expression, with its meaningful words, thoughts, stanzas, intentions, and actions. We also worked through the practical aspects of singing Musical Theatre such as the craft of the music and maintaining good vocal health. Let's take another look at the concept map from the Introduction and see if it now makes more sense (Figure 0.1).

I hope this is now more meaningful for you. If it is, it means your own network of concepts has developed and strengthened. This will continue, as you sing more, work with different teachers and professionals, and perform in more productions. You will probably find your map looks different to mine – that's great. Singing is very personal and we all have our version of it and a technique for realising that version.

Have another look at the procedure map, as well (Figure 0.2).

Impression–Expression: singing is simple as that.

I wish you all the best with your singing, now and for the future.

100 Final Thoughts

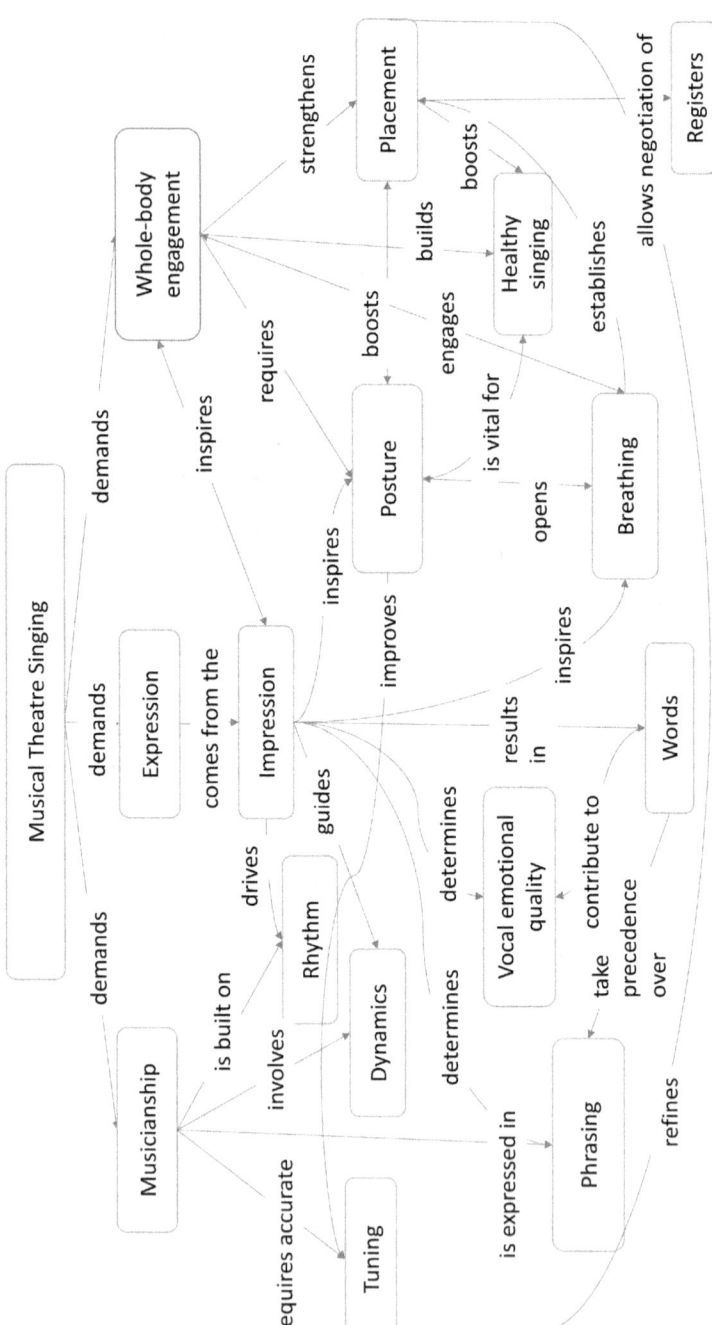

Figure 0.1 The network of singing concepts in the mind of the expert singer.

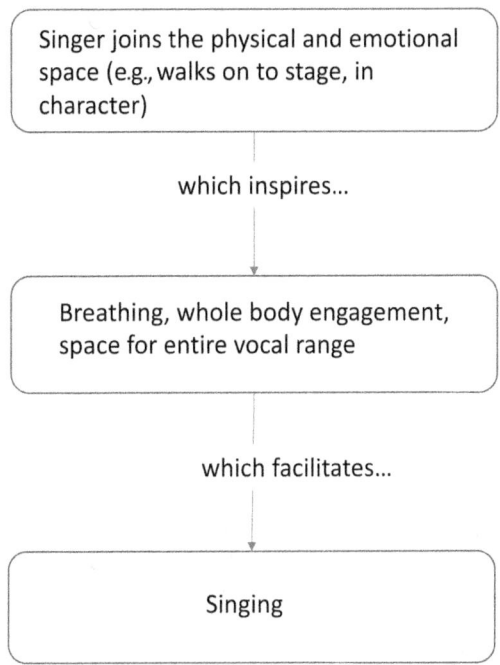

Figure 0.2 The "chain of procedure" of the expert singer, in performance.

Index

Note: Page references in *italics* refer to figures, in **bold** refer to tables and with "n" indicates endnotes.

absolute time 84
acting 14, 71, 83–87
Acting for Singers (Ostwald) 69
The Actor and the Target (Donnellan) 68
air flow 25, 26–27
air pressure 19–20, 25–26
Alexander, FM 7–8, 20
Alexander Technique 8
The Alexander Technique for Musicians (Kleinman and Buckoke) 8
Allen-Martin, Tori 71
Amelie 80
Anastasia 50
anatomy of breathing 18–23; air flow 25, 26–27; air pressure 19–20, 25–26; breath exercises 20, *21*; *see also* breathing
anchoring 12–13
appoggio 17, 20; exercises 23
Audition (Shurtleff) 71, 86
Austin, Stephen 25

beats 76–77, 79, 99
Bel Canto: A Theoretical and Practical Vocal Method (Marchesi) 32
belting: breathing technique for 45; earliest belters 43–44; exercises 48; overview 43; science behind 45–46; sensations and techniques of **47**; for singers 46–50; singers views on 46–50

Benson, Jodi 44
Blake, William 84
Block, Stephanie J. 44
Bogart, Anne 82, 90
Boggess, Sierra 36
Boleslavsky, Richard 76
Bowles, Sally 77
breathing: action of taking breath to sing 23–24; appoggio 17, 20; co-ordinating voice and 24–28; lutte vocale 17, 22; with placement 42; and rib cage 18–19; for singing 16–29; technique for belting 45
Brook, Peter 67, 70, 91, 94
Broschi, Carlo 22
Buckoke, Peter 8
Bülow, Hans von 95

Cabaret 77, 95
chain of procedure 2, *4*
Chaplin: The Musical 44, 83
Chapman, Janice 27
character 83; history 77–78; and Impressions 75–76; and songs 82–83
Chenoweth, Kristin 16, 39
chest voice 31, 32, 33, 35–36
Cinderella 97
Citron, Stephen 14
classical music 95
clavicular breathing 10, 18
Collela, Jenn 44
Collins, Billy 98n4

Company 96
composer and singing 95
cricothyroid dominant 33
Csikzentmihalyi, Mihalyi 70
CT dominant *see* cricothyroid dominant

de Alcantara, Pedro 14
"Defying Gravity" 44
DeMaio, Barbara 26
Dench, Dame Judi 67, 95
Dimon, Theodore 7, 10, 19, 24, 38, 41, 49
The Director's Craft (Mitchell) 76
Donnellan, Declan 68, 71, 73, 75–76, 78
dynamic tension 14

Erivo, Cynthia 44
events 76–77, 79, 99
expertise, defined 2
expert singer: "chain of procedure" of *101*; network of singing concepts in mind of *100*
Expression 79–87; notes on acting 83–87; songs and character 82–83
Expression exercise 81
Expressive Singing 1, 67, 68

Fantine 68
Farinelli 22; *see also* Broschi, Carlo
Farinelli's Exercise 22
fine tuning 51; *see also* tuning
Finishing the Hat 92
Fosse, Bob 14
Foster, Sutton 44
four-register system 33
The Four Voices of Man (Hines) 27, 31, 37

Gerber, Adam 71
Gershwin, George 43
gestures 83, 85
"Getting Married Today" 96
Girl, Crazy 43
good posture 7
Grace, Leslie 45
Great Singers on Great Singing (Hines) 17

Hall, Karen 10, 19–20
Hartley, Naomi 56

head placement 42–43; *see also* placement
head voice 31, 32, 35, 36, 42–43
Hemsley, Thomas 11–12, 13, 69, 80, 85
Hey, Mr Producer 67
Hines, Jerome 13, 17, 24, 27; on placement 37; on voice registers 31
humming 38–39, *39*
humour 83, 85–87
hydration 55–59

"I Dreamed a Dream" 68
"If You Hadn't, But You Did" 96
"I Got Rhythm" 43
illness 62–63
Impression: beats and events 76–77; character history 77–78; impact on character's obejective 75–76; maximising 71–74; and pictures 71; value of external focus 70–71
in-breath 23–24
Indirect Procedures (de Alcantara) 14
"In My Dreams" 50
In The Heights 84
Isley-Farmer, Christine 8–10

Jesus Christ Superstar 84
Journal of Singing 46, 63

Kander, John 95
Kayes, Gillyanne 12–13
The King and I 84
Kleinman, Judith 8

Leahey, Helen 35
Lindsay, Kara 45
The Little Mermaid 44
A Little Night Music 67
Little Women 79
Love Never Dies 36
lutte vocale 17, 22

MacDonald, Audra 16, 36, 39, 44
Mackintosh, Cameron 67
magnetism 85–86
Mamet, David 78, 93
Mancini, Giambattista 31, 89, 91
Marchesi, Mathilde 32
marking 62
medium voice 32

menstrual cycle: effect on voice on 60–61; irregular 61
Menzel, Idina 44
Merman, Ethel 43
metronome 95–96
Miller, Patina 36
Miller, Richard 22, 62
Milnes, Sherrill 17–18
Minelli, Liza 44, 95
Miss Saigon 89
Mitchell, Katie 76, 77, 84
mix-belt 41–42, 44–45, 49, *50*
mixed voice 32, 35, 36
mix-sung 44, 49, *50*
Motown the Musical 97
music: classical 95; Italian terms 97; rhythm 95–96; singing and composer 95; singing and musical phrase 93–94; song, beginning 94; and stage 92–93; styles 96–97
The Musical from the Inside Out (Citron) 14
Musical Theatre styles 96–97
The Music Man 84
My Fair Lady 80
mystery 85–87

The Naked Voice (Stephen Smith) 25, 27, 33, 37
Nesmith, David 8, 9
network of singing concepts *3, 100*
Newsies The Musical 80

objectives 75, 89, **90**
O'Hara, Kelli 16
O'Hara, Paige 44
Oklahoma 84, 96
"On My Own" 68
onsets 28
onset scale *28*
On the Art of Singing (Miller) 62
Ostwald, David F. 69, 74, 85, 91

painkillers and singers 63
panting 21–22
Parade 80
"Part of Your World" 44
passive pressure 25
Pavarotti, Luciano 59

performances: and humour 85–87; and magnetism 85–87; and mystery 85–87
physical noise 85
pictures and Impressions 71
The Pirate Queen 44
placement 37–40; breathing with 42; defined 37; elements of 38; exercises 38–40; head 42–43
playing: opposites 84; time and place 84
posture: diaphragm 10–11; feet 8; head 8, 11–12; larynx 11; legs 8–9; neck 11–12; pelvic floor 9–10; rib cage 11; and singing technique 7; trunk 10–11
Practical Reflection on the Figurative Art of Singing (Mancini) 31
"Precipice" 77, 93
Premenstrual Vocal Syndrome 60
primitive impulse 69
pubescent female voice 26

Ragtime 36
reflux 57–58
registers 31–32
relative time 84
resonance: exercises *39*; types of 40–42
rhythm 2, 82, 95–96
rib cage 7–8, 10, 16, 22–23, 25–26, 40; and breathing 18–19; and lutte vocale 17; and whole-body singing posture 11
Rice, Kathy Kessler 32
Roll, Christianne 46

Salonga, Lea 44
Sataloff, Robert Thayer 63
science: behind belting 45–46; and singers' training 1
Seiler, Emma 31–32
Semi-Occluded Vowel Tract (SOVT) exercise 58
sensation 1, 10–11; descriptions of **47**; and head placement 42; of relaxation 24; of resistance 27; and sound 43; vibratory 37, 39
Shneider, Christine 9
Shurtleff, Michael 71, 73, 75, 80, 84, 86–87, 94

simultaneous onset 28
Singing and Imagination (Hemsley) 12–13
Singing and the Actor (Kayes) 12–13
Smith, Stephen 63
Something Rotten! 80
Sondheim, Stephen 74, 92
songs: beginning 94; and character 82–83
sound: defined 1; emotional 1; and sensation 43; thick fold 33, 45; *see also* voice
The Sound of Music 83
So You Want To Sing Music Theatre (Hall) 10, 19–20
Spivey, Norman 48
SPLAT breath 27
"the stakes" 75–76, 79, 99
Stanislavski, Konstantin 16, 76
static tension 14
steaming 58
Stephen Smith, W. 25, 27, 33, 37
Steyn, Mark 14
straw exercises 58–59
Streisand, Barbara 44
Sunset Boulevard? 84
support 17; *see also* appoggio
Sydney Conservatorium of Music 60

TA dominant *see* thyroarytenoid dominant
tension 13–14; dynamic 14; static 14
testosterone 60–61
text **74**, 76, **90**, **92**, 94, 95–96
text exercises 89
Thibeault, Susan 56
thick fold sound 33, 45
thin fold 33

thyroarytenoid dominant 33
thyro-arytenoid-*dominant* (TAD) 48
Titze, Ingo 51
transduction 67
True and False: Heresy and Common Sense for the Actor (Mamet) 78
tuning 51–52
Two on the Aisle 96

unvoiced consonants 20–21

vocal health 55–63; effect of menstrual cycle on voice 60–61; hydration 55–59; illness 62–63; marking 62
vocal modes **34**
vocal range 34–36, 44, 48
voice 31–53; belting 43–50; and co-ordinating breath 24–28; head voice 42–43; and menstrual cycle 60–61; placement 37–40; registers 35–36; resonance 40–42; tuning 51–52; whistle tones 52
voiced consonants 20–21

West Side Story 75
whistle tones 52
White, Andrew 48
whole-body engagement 49; appoggio 17, 20; lutte vocale 17, 22
Wicked 44
The Witches of Eastwick 96
Wonderland 44
words 89–98
"Words, Words, Words" 96

Your Body, Your Voice (Dimon) 7

Zeami (playwright) 82

For Product Safety Concerns and Information please contact our EU representative GPSR@taylorandfrancis.com
Taylor & Francis Verlag GmbH, Kaufingerstraße 24, 80331 München, Germany

www.ingramcontent.com/pod-product-compliance
Lightning Source LLC
Chambersburg PA
CBHW071408290426
44108CB00014B/1733